Time Taken

By the same author:

The Vanguard Sleeps In (Glandular, 1981)
Cannibals (Rochford St, 1985)
Tickle (Island, 1993)
Nitty Gritty (Five Islands, 1997)
The Ways of Waves (Sidewalk, 2000)
Appetites of Light (Presspress, 2002)
Stories of the Feet (Five Islands, 2004)
The Ambrosiacs (Island, 2009)
Shadows of the Read (Ukrainian - Krok, 2011)
Barking Wings (PressPress, 2013)
Sea of Heartbeak (Unexpected Resilience) (Puncher & Wattmann, 2013)
El Asombrado (Spanish – Rochford St, 2015)
Getting By   Not Fitting In (Island, 2016)
Belief (Flying Islands, 2019)

Time Taken

New and Selected

Les Wicks

I don't drink
and I don't smoke.
I don't wear no crazy coat.

All we want are the facts, ma'am
Sgt Joe Friday

Someone I loved once
gave me a box full of darkness.

It took me years to understand
that this too was a gift.
Mary Oliver

All is chaos under the heavens, the situation is excellent.
Mao Tse-tung

PUNCHER & WATTMANN

First published in 2022, 2nd edition 2024
Published by Puncher & Wattmann
PO Box 279
Waratah NSW 2298

info@puncherandwattmann.com

NATIONAL LIBRARY
OF AUSTRALIA

A catologue record for this book is available from the National Library of Australia

ISBN   9781922571267

Cover design by David Musgrave

Cover art image "Trying to Save the Fishes" © Marije Berting

Printed by Lightning Source International

For Jennifer Wicks & Lynn Clayton

Cover image
https://www.deviantart.com/marijeberting

https://pixabay.com › users › marijeberting-890081

Contents

Touched

Landed

Water Ways

Puzzled

Peace

KEY:

New

Belief (Flying Islands, 2019)

Getting By   Not Fitting In (Island, 2016)

El Asombrado (Rochford St, 2015 in Spanish & English)

Sea of Heartbeak (Unexpected Resilience) (Puncher & Wattmann,2013)

Barking Wings (PressPress, 2012)

Shadows of the Read (Krok, 2011 in Ukrainian & English)

The Ambrosiacs (Island, 2009)

Stories of the Feet (Five Islands, 2004)

Appetites of Light (PressPress, 2002)

The Ways of Waves (SideWaLK, 2000)

Nitty Gritty (Five Islands Press, 1997)

Tickle (Island, 1993)

Cannibals (Rochford St Press, 1985)

The Vanguard Sleeps In (Glandular Press, 1981)

Poems marked with a QR code have a
musical/performance/video component.
They can be accessed through this code.

Hungry

One can find truth in a bottle,
but the light's a bit distorted.

L'Hôtel sur la Plage

In the first week at Stephen Street the cockroaches crept under the ivy-covered walls & nibbled harmlessly about the floor of our cool, shadowed kitchen.

Something happened, some dictator or new religion, because they became militant. By the third week there was a sign over our sinks saying *L'Hôtel sur la Plage*. Entire families lounged around the dripping tap, some using spoons as deckchairs. Juliet came in around midnight, turned on the light. Usually the brown plague ran for cover, this time only a few teenage topless roachettes at the far end of the sink seemed caught unawares. The rest just put on sunglasses & stared. A carving knife fell to the floor. Juliet got the point.

The next morning our garbage bin was full of insecticides, roach powder & our only flyswatter. A loaf of bread was missing, they'd eaten all our dope plus half a flagon of Riesling had gone.

Over the weeks matters got out of hand. We had to buy double quantities of groceries. *We're all on the dole!* I pleaded but it made no difference. By now some of the roaches rode on the backs of funnel web spiders & their leader had saddled up a baby tiger snake.

Fortunately, I missed the final battle. A bus (the driver distracted by a German Brown) ran me over & I was in hospital for a month. By the time I got out the nasty insects had changed the lock on the door & everyone had moved out. We're living in a park now, it's pretty good but jeez the mosquitoes are a hassle.

Trip

The road is a flat slimy black like
liquorice licked & stretched for weeks on end.

My hand on hop
waiting as shadows evolve to night.
We're at a great Australian bite
bittensmittenkittens drunken rosy
tired & toesy
silver taxi
& Van Morrison like a dim honey.

My job, blazing shirt & neat long socks,
is to collect the shavings of time.
Rain is the beat between songs
& I long

(but that's of little matter) slide past/
rubber on a futon.
Trees hang crucified with damp.
Bus stops & public toilets —
hordes of homeless crowd any shelter, their
tattered pennants concede in the pre-dark.

You raise a nailpolished hand
like a greeting (or salute). I don't care,
the cab just weaves over to your bags,
shuffles the downpour.

I've made you speedy — can't understand why.
Sharing this new address with me is an intimacy:
I know more than your workmates,
more than the authors
whose bedside books have brought tears & belly laughs.

There is some nervousness
inevitable
when one meets one.
Don't worry, I take what is required
(we could travel the scenic route
but would never arrive).

As the car leaps like a dolphin
to corner *Hampton & Hornsby*
Bel
rose

you explain
why this day is so sick,
so damaged.
How marriage, seemingly coated
in layer upon layer of waterproof varnish,
simply failed in a morning storm —
left puddles the colour of bruise
all over the driveway.

Plus your body — constructed in good faith —
is breaking down/
smart TV ads but no warranty/
impotent arrogance of the mechanics,
tedium of this tollway.

I laugh & disagree.
Corners turn, disappear like friends.
You lifted your hand to **me** — I
am charged   a knight
to the honour, the display of **any** trip. Your driver.

This is the street. That journey wasn't hard —
all your problems will either dry out

or wash away.
Have a fine evening. My touch,
like yours,
is either wind or stone.
We both lie down together
in the net of fallen hours.

The Hinge

Silver whistles slept
trains had abandoned
that brittle underlife.
In the empty waft of untapped electricity
he was somewhere up the way
& I, Safeworking Station Assistant Grade 2,
in my plastic-bucket-blue uniform
was afraid.

Smell of cooked asbestos, doused
under compacted seashell.
Existance is a rumour.
The doppler rose of passing trains & tripped signals,
this is the rationed blood
of these desiccated, invert worms.
Those tunnels need passage,
stainless steel is the lubricant. Absence
makes each surface scabbed & achy.
Rails flex — bereft, shackled.

There are the contrails, revenants of conversation.
People throw them out & they are trapped beneath ground.
Unfilled chambers mumble until dawn;
their uneasy dreams are ringtones, unfinished splinters of work,
break-ups, trick-savage plots or fashion.
I was always quiet as I wandered there.
We who walk the vacancy don't dare feed this sullen cacophony.
Speech should be collected as soon as it's spent —
like a confetti parade tailed by streetsweepers.

Tinctured air, I was infected & healed in stasis.

Emergency phones had been taken off the hook —
a systemic dysfunction, nerves jacked clacky.
Repeatedly,   over weeks. He or them?
Again that night, 3am, somewhere in the
underground
near my (lost my) Control Room.
Therapeutic cigarettes, cooling coffee.
I was off, *to effect an arrest.*

There was reason to fear —
a regular visitor the Lithium Lithuanian
sat in silence & waited for no train.
Also "met" George on the platform... the hairless
armless psychopath giant who wore a vast floral dress
so he could piss & shit unaided.
Sly aged Peter too, loved his god
or any little children left unsheltered.
These brittle islands above the flow of scratchy girl-less gangs
with all the hate that Saturday had thrown up all
over their denims.

Mere passengers can't notice
that rail stations swim in edgy, dirty data.
Inhumed, through the throat of night,
high tide of void
jetsam ribs of fluorescent illumination
so my feet
are about the dustdaisies
as rats chyme through vacancy
hung out on a city line.

Ozone frisson. Movement up ahead —
be a false alarm —   my torch (a weapon)
made its own burrow
at the end of which one figure
in aimless twist, the shaky wrist of this contact.

We each faltered, resisted
the hungry grunt of drains,
dual foci
two luminous flares of flesh.

No weather here, light is obliged to huddle.
But there's water —
forgotten fonts consecrate this narrow biology
that never eats sunshine.

Cabling fretted
in the pancake of stale air.
Hives of dark swarm the distance.
To approach a man like this —
flensed eyes flensed fingers flensed feet in flipflops —
shredded sphere of timetables.
He was what they called a *NFA*,[1]
owned nothing (I take even this story as my own)
my "arrest"   (simple as shunter gloves), think
I said five words,
barely registered in the dreary noise of his untreated mind.
He is caught. I am caught. Our roles
will not stretch. Power turns tale &
cleverness is no salve.
Beneath the rooves of cloud, six layers of time
cellophane of night & our practice being
what we're called. No choice
(the usual excuse).
He was put down
on a stalwart vinyl chair at the security office,
this bent & filthy hope.   The police
smashed his head
into an efficiently grey desk.

---

1 NFA — no fixed place of abode

One of them, blocky blond & aerated with action
asked if I wanted *a go*...
I was strong enough to decline,
starling twitch,
weak enough not to intervene.
Used my excuses frantically —
the hour (still in concrete catheters, the veins of night)...
there was no rehearsal.
All our days are numbered
moral failure   impotent vicinities.
Rills of snot,
NFA leaked scared & crying —
the constables thought they had a simple solution,
No point laying charges with fucken NFAs
YOU will never (bash)   *come to Central* (bash)
AGAIN (bash).
Another moment caromed past,
into the linger of weight
like stone above air, late shift lives on lines.
Still or in flail,

our culpable hands.

Prospectus

We chew away mountains —
earth is a rind.
The stars in the stone
feed our hungers of bone.
What remains?
The asteroid life,
mullock & lead dust.
Stay positive,
radioactive.
Our future glows like a cough in the murk.

The Code

In untidy light
criminals bud
on manky branches Singapore, London.
Ayn Rand's underpants smoulder
as sturdy factory workers are buried with their will.

Healing via austerity, Orchard Rd
(bypass pity). Five tattoos.
Those summer clothes
pass this merry chaos with
a chalky insouciance...
their carefree hip switch.

Each leaf is personal.
That same forest gives both fruit & outrage.
The cat farms an acre
we won't feel release
until the claws dig in.

Cry

1.
No leaves on the eucalypt outside,
a small splash of fresh blood on the doorstep.
The doorbell was a squeal.   "Party".
On that first night,
because I suggested
she took my hand & we went deeper into
the Wounded House.

After a moment,
Tammy shook off her top
sniffed at my praise
like tainted meat.

A brand high on her thigh
the smallest scar, the brightest art
under that ash-grey ceiling.

I stared out into the courtyard
pigeons & mynahs
are birds in the same game deck
of peck
& struts even the sun
mounted the privacy screen.
Pleasure is complex.

The truck driver wandered in like
some 'sixties missing link wearing
a towel & a handlebar moustache.
He smiled encouragement as I pumped from behind.
We are rendered
to half formed statuary. Elementals.

Handlebar awaited his turn.
We were all wounded.
Pleasure is work.

Without tailors & paint
each is exposed.

Jelly, gristle
injuries   body hair.
Skin is loose   there are tattoos
                 sleek
with freckles   both aroused & languid.
Well-known lawyer opened thin arms   batwing cloak
to the plum a troubled doctor has become.

Like us all
sometimes teased open.

Someone said *drink* we
queued for minutes.
Are you honey, wine or bile?
Fish escaped from my lips.

Someone said *eat* we
nibbled quietly as small scavengers ever will.

Like moulting birds, quiet on their branches
two large blondes (could be sisters) shed their layers.
A doddered geezer watched
with a cat's fixation.
His back was a mass of bruises   burns
& tiny cuts from the previous week in this place.
That damp patch could have been his Friday night.

What brought us
arms, bellies, eyes & legs?
What took our clothes
this bare mattress / xanthic light /
wooden frame sometimes
tight security surrounding no rules?

Playground where our own abuse
is the point of the game. But still
the **wonder**
our found extremity.

2.   Because she suggested
Handlebar took her hand
& led her to the wall.

The sisters
were vicious on the couch
with teenagers humping scared
on their toes.

Because I suggested
Tammy led me to the frame.

They hammered me
like a nail

until I was a part of the joinery,
the plaster of the Wounded House.

We Made It, It Made Us

Left the trees
& the junk beast rode us into town.

These houses! Such shelter, rain must hate it here.
We dread the monster but feed its puppies.

Cute as bottletops they snarf down anything that moves.
Amidst stainbows of discarded shopping bags
our life is sealed.

Staunch as dumped fridges, bright as tyrefires
we can depend. Must depend.

A genus of mountaineer, we create our own mountains
with garbage. Last season's *essentials* are flags at the pinnacles.

These peaks will last forever —
our legacy, our proof.

Serrated fingertips wake me up.
Sunday talks but I'm distracted by the blood.

Here in the herd there's so much busyness
who has time to catalogue predation?

The Compound

They gave her the keys
our community, this gaol.
We shuffled before her, a chain gang
or a gang of chains that tied this warden down?

She ignored the venoms of certainty
there was no restlessness
change loitered by the gates
but recidivism was high.
Walls protect & imprison concurrently.

> From the mouths of liars
> chaos tastes of cyanide
> freedom is belladonna.

They gave him the keys,
it was his turn. He lost track of the crimes.
Camp doctors ignored the gapes of injury
fussed instead around bunions & sniffles,
manageable matters.
There were dollars everywhere if you chose to look.

> Casino, parliament or gallery
> a hospital or school
> if you build a wall
> what's inside it makes sense.
> It just *has* to
> for all our sakes.

_ஐ_

Called Out

This is Cabramatta Station/
a low buzz, mumbled ultraviolet
Saturday night.
Crossing the pedestrian overhead
I've had 5 approaches:
Can I help you?

Tiny, well dressed & formal...
this is a powdered night for the busy youths,
vendors of small packages.

While down below
backlit public toilet purple
electricity's shadow
platform 1
users wait for trains in downpipe-drip silence.
Two security guards in nurse mode (white shirts ablaze)
keep the punters quiet & upright.
   They're built like
   & they are
   human bulldozers.

But the scene is almost as amicable
as the innocuous wallpaper of
Can I help you? A grey-haired shift worker
eats enormous steaming cobs of corn.
He's ravenous, but this is tonight's only
emotional excess.

This system so smooth,
progress so paved that

the rails are not steel,
any dream is beyond movement
at the edge of light.

Spin the Bottle

On the train
the two of them are big, wear
denim like animal skins, hair carved freeways
& beards a wilderness. They stink (soil, damp & sweat).

Talking to a woman
Newtown   mid 30s
her language cranked down to a Strine
that soothes, dampens, lubricates
the rambling of these men.

Everything they do or say
is as though it's grabbed.
Even simple talk about the weather is found
& taken like a ram raid.

No, she doesn't drink
after 15 years of fighting it —
Fucks ma head.
Her face torn,
tense — maybe unfriendly except for the words plus
she's given them her address
(causing the shit-rich shipwrecked
suit-woman across the aisle to become panicky,
a shiver at the perimeter).

Yeah Newtown. They're heading to the Cross...
for a while.

Realise they're me, bar a few accidents.
I'm her with her habits
in handbags & other people's hallways.

They're a miracle of matching
& so common.

Or rape. Will the guys talk about
sharing the bitch?

Perhaps she'll tame
& pamper them with hot meals beside eastern curtains.
Give them perfumed baths, stories to carry
to the next stop.

Prison, psych hospitals
the bush & the beats.

They're dangerous

& wander uncertain paths with only
a spinning bottle for a compass.

Angry

I have failed at that clean certainty
which lubricates all the greater hates

Her Light Fruit Cake[1]

Service is love dressed in work clothes.
— eastern suburbs Anglican church billboard.

Tracksuit, no make up
a gold wedding band snapped around a nail-bitten finger
I marvel as she swings up a solid arm towards
cordial on the top shelf at Go-Lo.

She's no part   of a new feminism, dabbles
as well as doubles   triples & more. So many modest roles that
just about makes one, her aim is for completion exactly like
in the 50's where the mother cooked
for family   neighbours   relatives
& family   neighbours   relatives until
occasionally she dropped in
a snippet of *Thall-rat*
& someone sickened.

Not even death the sometime goal, maybe
respite via husband's illness or a bald patch
on a wife-beater's head as she COOKED.
His till it's hers/ hymns to the hearse.
Either young, staunch as a new paling fence or
the worn-patch version of same.

Mrs Grills, den mother of the neighbourhood
or Mrs Monty poisoning her lover/son-in law we
take any woman for granted at some peril.

---

1 In 1950's Sydney there was a rash of domestic poisonings — so endemic
that a popular rat poison brand had to be taken off the market. Mrs Grills &
Mrs Monty were two of the most notorious poisoners.

A rough goddess' hand flips pages
of the washed-tone *Women's Weekly*.
At six fifteen each man clutches his beer
& stares at this night's dangerous plate.

La Dole Cheque Vita

You're born, there's no choice of posting,
it's the ultimate conscription.
Franz tries hard, burns candles at both ends
& by thirty he's the amateur firefighter
trying to kill the flames.
Rule One:
Live your own cliche.

Even as a baby he hoarded toys.
Rule Two:
You may as well enjoy your appetites. No one else will.

Good middle-class background
(work your way down).
Born with a silver ashtray in his mouth,
stuck at the bottom now, seeks shade
when it's *everywhere*.

Rule Three: Everything stuffs you up.

Franz lives the sweet life, still
dares to care at least weekly & hates
most of us for a good reason.

> Kookaburra sing.
> Kookaburra dance.
> Another hopeless case.
> Life at the steering wheel/
> ecstatic imbeciles ... *fringe dwelling man*.

Fix

Stop the fret   fight the war.
We repeatedly pick them up, those contentions.
I've seen bloody words shed
over words, language. There were
benedictions vs a poem. One sunset in the real world
boats just sailed on by, ignored —
the millionaires & migrants all bobbing away
from the swells of conflict.

If we are more than gristle & fluids
we must stand up, engage.
Was once friends with a warrior —
her parents were *disappeared* in Chile,
taught self-defence for women south London.
Sofia argued peace with readiness...
I was too awed to argue, maybe wouldn't have anyway
though where are the fists that do not crave use?
Open hands can also speak.

Her busy eyes, the unchained curls,
a laugh that painted the room. Judgement
was delivered in a tone drop,
that caustic ink of verity
which burnt through all the arguments
of voyeurs & thinkers like me.
She was unbreakable.
So poked around my own hate box,
inexplicably more cluttered than hers.
Couldn't see past the ramparts of small injuries —
both global & internal.

How much pacifism is cowardice?
Does intelligence dictate trepidation?

I show off scars
but they're mainly self-inflicted.
Will come to the day
when drowning seems less effort
than the constant strokes.

Before that may I chance to finish the hatings,
that bitter snack I've munched at periodically.
Don't care is saying too little,
asking too much.

Grimm

As the sun came creeping up like one big headache I had a piece of chicken.

Once free from its paper bag it just disintegrated, beaten down & weary after too many bashings & burns.

Back on the same some streets it's the first drunk-on-all-night for quite some time. Momentarily this is pure fairy-tale — all love, danger, both.

Throw the evacuated chicken bones to the gutter. They skitter towards the drain.

I glimpse (down there) something.

A street sweeper (stoop-scratch broom) muscles down the way. Those gutters resist like an ancient cranky hobo, his hair forcibly brushed in this bleak morning by un-caring combs.

Indignities multiply as a council truck sprays water but just the cigarette butts drown & sputter. This quiet is a sham.

A car loses control as the city wakes to preen itself.

Humans scuttle, we're apex insects.

He Did But See

Donald Robert Douglas
is an eminent writer. We know
because he brings along reviews
every visit.

He has no time for the children
& is often rude to our friends...
Artistic People are such scamps!

We find all these occasions
memorable.
Our only regret is that we have a mirror
right beside our toilet. In the turn
to persistent self-examination he misses
the porcelain point of the exercise.
Discover our floor awash with puddles.

Mary once raised the issue discretely.
His eyebrows were conspirators as they snuck together.
Theatrically offended he announced
the essence of earth
is dirt!
But we still grow weary
of poet's piss.

Pretend Tough

Need. To be. Hard.
Last week in a ruthless winter
with rain slicing sunrise
they cut away my bits, the ribbons of minor cancer
just a nip's worth of skin almost no blood.
This is weight loss for ageing beachbums.

So happy
gird the lions
as another species is excised.
Seen friends die
or worse live to be shadows.
Watched relationships bleed out with barely a tear,
seen kids taken from *difficult* parents.

Sheltered beneath the pout
of a grand financial institution,
two homeless guys get a barely wince.
Psychstorms wash out brilliant careers
cops circle like blowflies about
the runny nose of need...
poverty of cash, poverty of crash.

Always been like this,
angel dust cakes to antique spoons.
I've got some stories too —
one of the new masters once pulled up,
I was interested as he fucked a teenage me.
Got some money & a ride home in
(yes a real) Cadillac.

Jenna

Mate, how many times I gotta tell ya.
Delinquent collapse of dyed blond
over rhyolite eyes
in this tarnished-silver train.
Hungry tar of a secreted cigarette,
"nice" passengers fret —
coughs emailed across the aisle.

I don't fancy ya.

Everyone listens, these two
have that amplified Strine
lubricated in beer
operatic slur.
Cowboy hats on/off & sunnies
frayed levis cinched tight by angry belts
another station passed
he tries a line
but flops.

I GOT a boyfriend n he'll bash ya/
n he'll bash me if he catches us.
Mid-afternoon, slipped in the week — a rules time.
The rest of us en route to appointments, small importants
beyond the yards. No worries, nothing too hard.
But they've had a day's worth
cock-sloppy strut.
I remember
the murky solace of empty morning bars…
tides asleep, long-back   long-neck.

Their narratives are scrawled in tattoo ink
his negligent mullet —
tight, tiny mouth fenced in stubble…

a trail of troubles.
They're both thin as fluorescent light
lunched on tinned complaint & shoulder chips.
Small time/ short time master, his psychiatrix.

We wuz drinking as mates but
yr no mate, mate.
Don't fancy ya.

I guess he bought the drinks.
Pension time   stumbling tongues
monosyllable hands.
They share a seat
with their brown paper bag.
Something about trains & darkholes...
snog towards Sutherland.
Finger slide on a pale spine —
our new prince.
Lost key, tiny plans
with grit
duration one hour.

No way mate.
Maaate.
Bob.

— like a deep breath
before a long dive.

Trouble

In a too exactly square room watch
myself in the mirror at the far corner.
The eyes
are smudged
I'm tired, tired on too little
an imperative to burn.
Turn off the music, then the light, draw
the curtains & hang a shirt over the mirror.

Contrived
like a ritual. The shirt doesn't work
I'm left looking at myself in the corner of the glass,
cut off, just like I wanted in blackness
& silence. Can't find the matches in the gloom,
can't even light a cigarette let alone
burn the world. Looking for something new, even fresh,
try my hardest — perhaps too hard.
I open one of the curtains.

Perhaps the Adventure

or maybe just the peacocks, their pecks. Paris, 1940.
Les Boches have lined up our Gauloises & shot them.
Plus, the internet hasn't even been invented.

Klaus thinks Feminism is all about the Jews.
Who said monstrosity can't be flexible —
those Aufseherinnen —
given a real job by clueless men but
Women in Uniforms, they get ideas.

As America undergoes a talking-to
intrepid British spies bugger each other
like tertiary educations.

Kristallnacht is a brand of champagne —
everything makes sense
if you forget energetically.
Pétain has been reading about Panama...
he has niggles over the mosquito problem, the heat
& when accosted by humidity
that way pianos so easily warp into jazz.

Paris must be preserved!
Think of all the movies to come
Hepburn, Marlon, Woody, Kate Hudson.

The last lies are progress.
81 years later
the Arc de Triomphe is fake news.
Ex-colonies simmer & refuse
those grand plans imposed on them yet again.
Such ingratitude, like malignant toffee
thank god it sticks in their throats.

Just Saying...

Love is the answer.
Try that argument
in the camp on the Turkish border.

Beneath American summers
a woman loses her mind.
Tax policy has made no difference
& healthcare, well, one has to laugh
or rage.

Every step I've taken
has been on stolen land, guilt builds
like soil formation & blood has always been
the best fertilizer so our crops shimmer.
Vitamins sizzle in the sun
as an ageing world dribbles.

We are carp, agasp on the banks
of the river of our own design.
Do I bite, bale
or just flap about uselessly?

This weekend, further up in the hills
hazard reduction.
Look down the valley
Perth wears the smoke like some kind of armour.
Like us all, yes it does inhale.

When the petitions arrive, I sign.
Many women move to overtake male extremity,
not a moment too soon.
Men are puzzled but there's a kind of way forward.
First People change all that needs to

& Bren is just what the component parts feel —
a person, untethered by gender.

Another march? Do we buccaneers
turn pamphleteer again? Brochures
are no less readable when soaked in tears.

This middle-aged carp won't refuse
any lifejacket offered.
With impotence as the new flag
we compose/decompose at a bright future.

News

Down King Street
my smoky pockets dance for this spring, stand
like a bridge between two ex-friends
when the shots began.

Assuming it to be another car noise I
amble on /\....
writing in the air, try
to remember some song we all recall but was not a hit.

Krak Mid burble notice others
down at the gutter or
hiding in store alcoves like a *no-junk* mailbox.

Krak It's as though a
new traffic light has appeared. Cars stop,
some drivers leave their cars at a run.
Engines hum like Buddhists under the night.

Krak Hit the dirt.
Chew concrete. This is deep genuflection.

Krak As we wait for police, ambulance & press,
(the busy trinity)
a man cradles his arm, bewildered.

Alongside him three women in tears.

Krak A very young female police officer pursues, returns fire,
clutching the heavy gun like a crucifix
while her male colleague stands behind the car with
as much presence as a table napkin.

It finishes. The crowd dusts off & congeals into
one gossiping mass.
Sixteen police cars, helicopters overhead.
The officer paces the asphalt (gun still out),
not connected to the others massing everywhere...
her youth lights bulbs along the
forced indifference of her profession.

I too have a tiny role, the
uneasy eye. Feel the words rise already,
barely aware of panic,
& drink
it in.

⬤

Heard from America

He has enough
& there's spinal pain like all bipedal mammals
then He has had enough.
Fat little outcomes
along his path to white middle-age —
all lost — or at least that which he now thinks
were most precious, most His.

He talks to Her online, fibre cooks the air.
So She is browbeaten down to agreement like
Her spinal pain this world is crooked, conspiracies
Her thinning hair tangles with airborne notions
of that life that is maybe lined with leather but those
couldas ran off like tumbleweeds.

The Couple discovered Lizard People
(who eat little kittens)
& those Jews in banking.
Surprised there is so much to say They
built a Network of Folks
who knew to blow in the direction of the wind.
So They are 7% now,
there was rustle on the radio
& guns remain relatively cheap.

Friends

People are like keeping
tigers for pets.
All big & cuddly
but ya might get et.

Little Imogen Black

is just a bit *creepy* when she cuddles him
(admitted only under this sanctity of paper).
In this foster-life so far six months
healed about delicate regulation that
relief of regular breakfasts, predictable nights with
no dangers behind her shoulders she
is allowed a childhood in the paradise of Telopea.
On her way
the daisy way
that only is seen
from a distance like love.
Imogen still *wants to die* in the crisp linen
on her burnished bed,
she keeps thinking back through the day
those *clean* smells. *Now*, not then.

> Ibis fly over the hill of fractured bones,
> do you throw away broken parents?
> Lions of the ratty lounge
> argued over teams & demanded.
> Boys will be monsters. *Then*, not now.

The sensualities of pizza
& future... a good girl, desperately attentive then
hugs so normal
but so many, there's a discomforting hunger.

Show & tell no bruises, a pantene flick of hair
then she is there.
Pack her lunch to
the novelties of school, St Bernadette's Primary
painless incarcerations maybe games, a friend ...
fierce, tiny ambitions so
flagrantly normal.

A spectator at the borders of radiance,
in the sun of her temporary family
she is ruled by an arthritic Labrador.
There can never be too much
of just now.
Our tumid world is smeared with the ichors of money,

but this costs nothing more than this.

Maybe It's Because I'm a Londoner

1.   Ratty parks where youths wait in rags
   for the chance of money.   No wizard here.

2.   **Crunch**
   I'd been run over & had a small operation. There were
   complications & I found myself stuck in hospital for three
   weeks, told later I could have died.

   & then when all this had edged away into a memory the famous
   poet walked in & showed me death in the palm of his hand as
   casually as if it were a new hobby.

3.   *The boy sat on the burning deck*
   Jules had left France to escape the draft & register for the dole
   in England. We'd become good friends. Together up the stairs
   to the fifth floor of the Wandsworth council flats (lift never
   worked). See the vast Battersea Power Station smoking on our
   left. Jade & Erica are both single mothers. Both play guitar. We
   sit in front of their television, they sing a couple of Cohen songs
   but can hardly be heard above the 9 o'clock news. Drinking
   wine, spaghetti Bolognese.

   Trains rattle the whole block as they take people out of London.
   The last movie begins, *An Affair to Remember*. The women sing
   Blueberry Hill as Cary Grant edges towards Deborah Carr. He
   says *I was worried for a while there were no beautiful women
   on board*. We go down to the pub for cigarettes & a few drinks
   before closing time.

   I win 50p on the fruit machine, Jade complained she got a split
   lip & a black eye down here last month. Back at the flat two
   small children sleep unattended.

A shadow play, Dave tries to be allusive while mauling pie & finishing his pint. He's expecting his wife to give birth at any moment… says he has to go home to check on "the woman" in a while… after the coffee, *ha ha*, at Jade's.

Coffee. Jade's kid wets his bed & screams. All of us regret the dope drought. Jules & I leave. Erica too. Dave's staying put, laughs at one of his jokes then rearranges his crotch like he's tidying it up for an expected visitor.

4.   *An Affair to Remember*

The night has become so drooled that even the traffic has died. Marina & I in a temporary kind of love that she calls *Bohemian Insomnia*. Whatever she says in that accent sounds fabulous. We never sleep when it's dark, just make love & prowl. See Thatcher's Britain as Germany in the 30s. Write stories for different magazines in different countries. Can't help but mention that London's in a mess.

5.   **Daffodils**

The cup of night is plastic & everything just doesn't taste right. We buy drinks on notice that another year has fallen into the sea. No one can agree whether people are still the same or changed irrevocably. Then months disappear. By April the weather eases & my fingernails reappear.

6.   **The Brixton Beat**

On the main artery, close by the Tube, a kid picks up a brick with the same bland violence that men of power can wield without consequence. Walter sits, watches the riots, on TV. His shift starts in an hour.

Constable Walter Egan walks through a light April drizzle with his cheek cocked close to the lapel of his coat speaking into the microphone. It's the drizzle that causes the hunched posture, not tension despite all the changes to the area over the last years. Those Blacks make it hard though, they ignore you. But there are still places where he could call in for a cuppa.

Eight till four, five days a week (earnt after 15 years of service) suits Walter just fine.

7.   Excuses

Jules: *Living the last generation we must still face all the important battles. Destroy desolation, self-love & obsession. We continue to fight for the right to be an individual, for the freedom of our art. Those that persist in these struggles are the generators which will power the future of the Earth & be the summation of all human positive energy in those decades before forever.*

Marina: *In years to come phenomena will create themselves — everything will be Tantric & people can fuck forever 24/7.*

Clapham Pirate

Raf's eyes sway around from
the fireplace like a leering crane
on a tiny wharf.

You can piss in the kitchen sink, Petey,
but if you don't turn on the tap
*it's **unhygienic.***

The smile was full of gaps/ /
post-apocalypse dentistry from the prison system.
Petey's father's friend
more pirate than any child could hope for.
He hung onto every word.

Howling winds outside
the communion of sweet tea & cakes.

He listened when told
All people are good
'cept screws
& pigs & grasses.

Raf's tattoos danced,
muscles snuck around their bones like burglars.
He could fix anything.
Dad & Raf were like a two-day party every
fourth weekend.

Custody was never in doubt,
Petey knew his dad & society were birds & worms,
only which one was which ever changed.

Come Sunday his return home to Mum was like
the end of day release.
But Raf explained that nothing matters *'Cept mates*
& Petey was beyond a fuss,
irrepressible in the London chiaroscuro.

Spirals

Wilma *travelled with the band*, rolled the pleasures & smiled.
The van stopped for me, 18th birthday.
I was dust, breeze   & invisible — Sunbury Festival, 1973.

She was *cool*, the guys were superstars
in a matchbox galaxy. I was almost speechless between gazing
at her gorgeous-reckless hairy calves
& the mandala of breast beneath Indian cotton.
I kinda write poems.

London 1982, Clapham squat, I
was *gonna make it* yeah, sure.
She'd never spoken to me in English, just French
which I'd picked up like a limp.
Then *Tu es également Australien?*
So many drugs, we'd met again,
celebrate over smoke,
she'd travelled with no money or dreams across a world.

Wilma was *amazing*, all
those kilometres had extinguished any possible home.
Some nights I'd just gape at her as she recited road stories —
that marvel, that hurt.
I have been lost.
Booked my flight back to Sydney.
There were many failures.

Gut Feelings

The city continues to burn, Thatcher riots. This feels like elastic crystal we step over the white stones. Bone sun. Red eyes. The people have been crying all night & Sunday afternoon seems hardly awake with all the sorrow it carries. I have no home so head off to friends. I know how to break in if no one is there, I feel I know how to break in even if there's no house. They have just fixed their television & it looks like, for me, a gruel London Easter or bust.

Months later back Sydney & burning forest is this shallow city's mane. Late afternoon, sun weird poled light & the brown corona of high energy. This is what Sydney does. We wait like babies in the parks, watch storm clouds in the west sit unmoved like a scoop of ice-cream in a mistake.
Scarlet sun   homeless.

The next day Angela takes me to her rooms & we're together again. 5×7×7 are the figures. I enjoy talking with her & just when I think we may be immortal she says
My breasts have stretchmarks.
            28? That's pretty good, your breasts are fantastic.
I wrap myself around her until she falls asleep then creep away from the house feeling like the child that escaped. Think *28 is **so** old.*

Must be alone. I sit in the park, mumble. I have a friend. Sit there like the lost ice cream. The night is light is alone.

A gentleman from the equator once said Angela was too hot for Australians. Perhaps he was right. A little hurt a little fear. Wait again for Angela to take me home. *Take me home.* Step out onto six lanes of traffic, head towards a homeless city of business. I run stupid panicked hungover... left in the riddle as the world turns/ as a chicken crosses the road. Why?

Anne

was Toby when we were last together in John's car,
watched the swatting of horrors from a crazy blade of hair
(that choice of movie,
not a good idea) the marijuana
was a blessing.

Emails come in from Mexico, manana trees. My friend
almost died after the gender realignment operation
but still gardens a dry-climate treaty with
fronds of fellow complexities, paints
out front of her gallery.

Not easy being a trans lesbian there.
The art is a blaze, saw
this cascade on a website. Anne's
girlfriend is *an identity*, not least
for those wings tattooed across her back.
Aloft, everyone, no decision.
That promise of cash & burn/
children play in the scars.

Happy Cup Sing. P/L

She was saying   *aw mate...*
since I got off the drugs me periods are real regular every month
that Sherri mate she's a real moll when she's got her periods,
wasn't at first though, real shy. I said, I don't wanna fuck ya, just
lick ya clit but she gets off goin' more I say get that tampon outa
ya n we go for it n mate n she's hooked.

I'm not dirty like, I stick some coke up ya nose when ya comin' but
I'll never cut ya up on a blade...

We are all wattle
beside the *Lucky Dragon Loan Office*
sugar covered
I only want to be with you.
Her parents came from
Somewhere Pacific.
Our train was rattled aluminium,
egg-custard bun sullen clown.

Sun is our property, constant
above multi-storey car parks
at multicultural suburbs.

Speaking as one in easy-fit denim
beside the *Hong Kong Wedding House*
watch dealers outside *Tang Bou Noodle Shop*
not interesting, we are wattle.
Decorous in array, barely a mention in singular
the illumination & the allergen
we are thin gold rings, unnamed fillets
on a shaved-ice seafood bed.
We are *Shopping Paradise,*
Gold Swan two-ply tissues

Amy Chan in concert
specials bin in the *John Street Arcade*
the glitter in passing hair
ao doi or trackpants/ugh boots
as explicable as a line of ibis,
their diagonal napkin-fold of sky.

This table display
of pink embroidered bras
is a greedy lake. On a carpet
of petty & repetitive sins
tea-candles, *Light of Wisdom* reduced to clear.

Today clouds write letters home.
My eyes are an acclamation of green plantains
beside the conflagration of coral trout.

Hymns should be bellowed —
give gods some ears & voice.
They will be the *Saigon Blade*
or that brave, snide 19-year-old Melanesian lesbian Ocker
in a well-mixed home town.
If she ever picked
or kicked you — you'd learn.

My poem is a comma on the freeway, empty freight beds
plump up alongside the Southern Line.
Writing here at the end of ordinary
where colours somehow blend.

Sky Trail

This one was
or was called
a witch perhaps. So she disappears, her
only trick.
Why travel? No *home*, (an inflexible, judged word —
foolhardy for any to claim) but she was there
a tough demountable equivalent.
Some can't tell the difference
up close
under torture your
head beneath a cruel, sanctified pond.
Her skin is her bag
& now flag.
Great western wings weigh down the air. Oddly cold
her fingers clutch documents they are
a calumny of worship against
labile ink   suspicious eyes.
Fear the war cry of these new clerks.
Given time
(that's a story).
The teacher & a cash register.
Some piteously
bright future. Which is taken…
we'll be surprised.

Colour & Movement

We all have our lists, those who
led us away from the routes so carefully planned.
The drunk guy on the train
said Daryl Somers[1]
had changed his life.

With a leer, like some kid's
first public magic trick

he said
Ya'll neva neva know, if ya neva never go?[2]
& he was then so
simply right.

Because that jingle had brightened those beery eyes,
all our attention wandered out through the glass
to bushland & beguiling clouds.
The day was crowded with decisions.

To be gone? To grab
or grind, the temptations beyond each back yard.

He leaned across the aisle,
told one of the women there
Ya've got a lovely smile darlin' —
what do ya do?

> *I'm a sister.*

Yeah, I've got a sister too.

> *No, like a nun.*

---

1 Once popular middle of the road TV personality
2 Theme for TV tourism ads featuring Daryl

But 30 minutes later it's
Neva neva know...
Got a boyfriend, luv?
& his mates are amused, embarrassed

while the woman's well-trained niceness
sits vibrantly starched.
Her tan linen placidity will not be shaken
by the flash of passing red-gum,
an effulgent spray of water over stone.
The bible on her lap
is some kind of anchor

as Daryl's regurgitated visions rattle us all
Parkes, Condobolin, Darnick, Menindee   due west.

Ho Ho Heil

On the station the aging Nazi skinhead
is just another baldy now, he's
finished his last minute Xmas shopping.
Poking out from his festive T-shirt
those swastika tattoos on his neck
have paled to a gunmetal grey.

Torn cotton shorts on a multicoloured rail station,
it seems like all his arguments
have been fought to exhaustion.
A smiling Moslem woman & her decorated pram pass,
Excuse me.

He carries a fist like some limp Kris Kringle
but there's no party left, his
festive ham sweats on the seat beside him.

Rejoice — like all the other energies, hate fades.
Let it rain, let it sour.
Mistletoe & other plastic celebrations are
relentlessly bright. He didn't say a thing.

But this is valued knowledge.
Children's feuds, the struggles in the queues.
History clutters up summer. This season of giving
hasn't given up. His phone rings,
a loving family reels him in.

Ward

The 75-year-old ladies' man is all cut up
in the hospital bed next to mine.

He loves his dog, brags he once slept with a woman
plus her 30-year-old daughter at the same time...

some sort of summit for him
& *they were both satisfied.*

He's lost most of the bowel, half his bladder, spleen,
appendix, bits of lung, a snip of the oesophagus,

prostate. Finished with a distal pancreatectomy. Reckons
he's now the ideal weight for his age. Great pharmaceuticals &
you've gotta hope. Because his kelpie[1] Jimmy is barely two,
wouldn't understand the blunt thievery of death.

Still got all his hair & a full pension
which is *accumulating nicely* while he's in the Royal.

Professor Coure is *happy* with the surgery
but hasn't been around much since.

There's a morphine pump & this cheeky Irish nurse.
Maybe he'll get up next week. For Jimmy.

---

1 Australian dog breed

Sheath

Each shell is a life's work & worth.
Made from sputum, memories
some dark-hard minor victories
glimmer at the edges like eyes
drunk on a pretence that futures are seen.
We two walk an overgrown riverside track.

I was right there man, I was offin' myself.

Crusts are worn like signature coats around town.
Dace — his casing had that extra shine last week —
a corona of clarity. Almost
hilarity. The decision had been made.

*I felt the tingle mate, told myself
that was IT.*

This carapace, it should have a weight.
Is certainly a burden each bears
though it corrodes, transforms.
Something to do with ingredients —
guilt & outrage kill slowly.
Struts are built of boredom,
that very human poison.

*Don't know why I fucken rung 000.
Don't know why I'm talkin' to you.*

Perhaps this process is a cocoon
though we carry it all our lives
there are rumours of 'emergence'. One can scarcely look
at these trails of abrasion, there's some promises —
those wild disfigurements of flight.

Alongside a watercourse we have so little to say.
Our struggle through reeds, insects tax us to white.
There are crabby sky-slits in all this pitiless miasma.
One foot forward
into *experience*. A channel of floozy water emerges up ahead;
a river births from chicanery. We will arrive.

Feel bloody great now mate, go figure.

Crash

Bernie McGann's sax looks like
Roman Empire plumbing. Its notes
erode sandstone/
shake trees in matchstick groves.

Sometimes it's a skanky garden fork
with scoops of weed, worms — gravity & squirm.
On a roll/
is on the dole. It's the niggling pain in the spine.

Terrifies the elderly
as brass rattles down pavements between
rush & a stumble.
Bernie McGann's sax
would growl at polish.

Old pine, ice cream highs —
outdoor jazz, obligatory early summer.
There is a conspiracy on stage
decided by a morse of grunts & finger.

McGann brushes clouds out of his reed.
He prowls above the band
waits for the solo
like some grinning bear at a fish farm.
Plastic seating hesitates, then
a shudder from the demountable platform. *Ugly Beauty*.

Damien Gives a Lesson

Cancer unfolds like
some lettuce in his brain.
A coal squats stolidly in the liver.
This afternoon a discussion on *palliation*.
There are clear answers to this quiz,
he scoffs at the notion of conquest
& plays guitar.

Despite a generation of ropes
we hold hands.
Despite a lifetime of hopes
say *you never looked better*.
I'm right.

a Few Problems

This couple's nest is made from shards
of tooth enamel & lightbulb-glass,
one egg has passed its use-by date.
Their souls are an omelette of salt & flawed ambition.

She in her corner, removed
from the imagined glare
of stick-figure enemies next door.

He has a chair built around his back problem \
/   wants all this life packed
      with such efficiency.

Twice a year they have sex, it's like bushwalking,
both wonder, yes,
must do more often.

There is a collection of
their car alarm memories on CD.
They no longer have a player.
The News is a scream.

Let's stay together
For The Children.

Suburban Fabric

The social worker in that
crisp summer skirt, her
smile flummoxes my block's usually
imperturbable security door as across the road
a swarm of arborists dissect the trees outside #35.

This suburb's ecology, perhaps
distanced from me. Complete
or marooned I take my pick each day.
Good neighbours build tall offences —
as we grow under glass the glow is our final reason.
Like blatant camellias we all mimic open,
our generosity, frail petals this cluster of life
each home composting
it is disaster, leakage & jewels
plus the bodies of our aged ones as
they falter across a line that exists, is maintained by

that social worker in the
crisp summer skirt, she's trained;
has a series of guidelines *Who's the prime minister?*
(we'd all rather forget). The stalks of the tiger lily
have their drum solo as stumps opposite are ground down
maybe those eucalypts were a *fall hazard*;
there're rules for that too like
that bikie in #29 his fat arrogant tyres abrade
the purchases of serenity. Another law is passed
& he sounds just the same. In #39 a new single mother
will smile at anyone. The hope (& plea) radiates so of course
we avoid being burnt. I tap on the skin of this community
they think they've let me in, some virus under the door
perhaps they have perhaps not, like

the social worker in that
crispness truly skirting the surface
of those incandescent spectacles
that make up each infected life.
My friend Ismat & I will visit the RSL
for jazz that's not quite cooked,
a seeping salmonella of riot down in the core. She
has a story that leaves me thirsty.
Her magnets have been busy, the orbits tease belief.
It involves, yes,

that social worker who turns out
to be madder than the rest of us put together.
Who was a doctor once. She didn't use pethidine she
fucked pethidine she married pethidine
they grew into their 30s together. Disqualified,
retrained, rehabbed... a re-tread
& lectures Imelda in #22 with a spasmodic fervour what
a lifesaver, she could tell you...

User Manual — Men

The trick in all this trickiness
is to deceive the nasty inner thing lodged
under our not-so-hardy skins.
Make sure we have access to tools, use
the river's suncut pills of tranquillity
& outboards. Perhaps
take us to our lovers.

Painting houses & epiphanies
there is always the excuse wrapped
in a criminal shrug. One long declining tide, our story
reveals wonders & desiccates simultaneously,
the horrible harmony of our aging.

Rules state blokes can hammer one item per day —
even just nailing an argument
means convulsion & guts. We never clean up afterwards.

Spit flies from the driver's side window
of a metallic green Mazda. There is male beauty everywhere
& trajectory within vapours. Men fearlessly remove
their fellow domestic pests — cockroaches, rodents.

We are a problem that is not insurmountable.
Should be managed with tolerance
& vigilance... advised on appropriate clothes or
counselled down to sensitivity (what we say is what we are?).
Don't accept excuses,
you are not them.

Take us out for a run, the north wind hurtling
laughter through our thinning hair.
We sing badly & rarely

but with great passion. Let us repair the shower screen.
Lead us to your pleasure.
We are better than cats
for most household camaraderies.

Touched

Everything
mucks you up.

Awash

Love is like the waters
yearning, powerless, led by the moon.
Eats the land, is eaten.
Evaporates, no matter how hard you try
just evaporates.

Oceans are scoured by indifferent nets.
You can get any answer
with a cloth & bucketful.
Boil some ardent potatoes
or hose down your post-separation sports car.

Even the criminal at the time of execution
should be treated with tender love

Young fingers stroke the epilimnion
of the lake where he was conceived.
A roughhouse wind tangles his hair —
a few drops sprinkled & the mother tames it back.
Horses watch fascinated
this grooming of the bipeds.

Get married, for I will boast
of your great numbers before the nations.

Common & unique
water is the mother of all fissures,
her sand the work of centuries.
No wall can withstand
our mistress of unmaking.
Life was an experiment she once tried
her feckless biproducts muck it up.

Because each religion is just a branch of love,
franchises love.

A witch was for dunking
as seas were "conquered".
The ships were fat scabs that wept garbage.
Peoples & species lapped up the toxins
while dreams sputtered
while phlegm flew.

In the end, only two things matter:
how much you loved,
and how gracefully you let go
of those so many outcomes not meant for you.

Yet still they talk of love, that stumpy-littered word:
starts with a shard, that javelin "l" then
gyre & blade to
a wet letter "e", the comber to finish.
Because that element always waits for the collapse
of conceit & delusion.
Waters rebel against any receptacle.

Servitude is love dressed in work clothes.

A latrine of deities,
holy men & women persist,
preach love as some emollient.
Far stronger, less predictable than any god
it is unanswerable...
as malignant & seditious
as truth.
Instead blame love,
         imprison the rivers
                  piss on the shoreline.

I still aspire...

surf above then within the wave
kneel, knell, inhale, sink.

Jo'n'wicksy

My first love's name was Joanne Taylor.
We were eight & she lived close by in one of
central Parramatta's remaining "slums".

Her mother had disappeared,
it was a dark
undiscussed secret
like murder & ghosts.

The father was a drunk.
Something known despite the fact
I always went home before he returned from
whatever.
We shared Joanne
& the bad-backed terrace in shifts.

In July the house still had
xmas stuff all around the walls.
Jo said it saved putting them up each year,
they'd become monkey bars for bugs.

There was no fridge.
Joanne said she *preferred* jelly to ice cream.

No television, me neither.
We'd sneak across at night to
WARD'S ELECTRICAL, join others
as the silent images flickered behind plate glass.
Promising much, explaining little.

That year Dad bought our HMV but Jo & I
would still meet at Ward's
              (my loungeroom cheapened

      television's
      quality of light).

At xmas the battle-scarred decorations got so right.
Summer jelly took longer to set,
rested on a shelf like something festively important.

I gave her a kiss (it seemed correct),
then said my family was moving to Dundas.

She shrugged in her practical clothes
& our search continued in the
archaeology of her back yard.

My first of hundreds/
incomplete goodbyes.

The Knife

I stabbed him when he tried to leave.

In bed together, her neat white underpants
& flesh coloured bra...
simple objects of intense concentration.

We scored the double bed as that
night's only couple,
feared or wanted destinies in our hands.

She said that, her hardest secret...
then tales of psych hospitals,
patients mewling, sexual abuse.
I only half listened, planned to delay
this body business for
perhaps a generation or so.

Her dad called her a boy's name
because she "wrecked" her mum being born.
He was a cop, only wanted sons.

Gave me *The Little Prince* a week later.
No nicks or scratches.

I so regret
that this is all I remember.
These scars have come
from knives less dramatic
than teenage pain.

Promise

For you
I'd fly to Iceland if I heard that you were free
for just one night & wanted me there.

For you
I'd find your brother a job
& look for one myself.

For you I'd buy a kite &
invent electricity.

I'd change my style stop
using my nose
eat healthy & miserable
put children in juicers
be one of the losers
a weight reducer.

I would invent electricity
with you
            blow us all up.

The Nurse

She'd been waiting a long time for the letter. The envelope was ripped open, discarded like the most insubstantial of enemies. It just sat on the floor with the other junk. Out of the picture now. You wouldn't know. You wouldn't know but her entire body was laughing at a joke on the fourth line. She keeps things in, there's just a sort of tick in her left eye & a hiss as she inhales.

Family news, neighbours back home, semi darkness, one lamp. Her boarding house room is in a mess. The letter is well spaced with every second line blank. It helps her mother get to the bottom of that obligatory, one sheet report. There is nothing new to say. These notes are simply ritual... give the other notice of continued existence.

The people at work think she's stupid. 12-hour shifts. & always afterwards (coming in past "No Visitors Allowed") there's old Mrs Waterson... usually a good word to say.

Karen has a compact record player & some favourite songs. The volume never gets too high, she joins in on the best numbers. Every week (this week late) that letter arrives. Each three months a visit back to the straight dusty street, familiar ground of Kurraga. She can say at least *that's behind me*. It's a sort of pride that eases. Karen hopes a little more & has a little less. The letter finishes "yours sincerely". She is in control. & smiles.

Finding Ourselves

Here on the beach it's rough justice
says Julie under a frangipani.

Coconuts grow on Main Street. The *vibe*
is re-used, even money looks travel worn...
thinner than the leaves.

Julie explains her escape, country freedoms.

I write, furtive as a flea
      The moon in the sky.
          (No images left,
            the moon is a public drink).

The woman made a fictional character called Julie.
She was to be a creative person living by the sea.

      The last myth I broke was me, then
      silence as loud as inconvenient death
      in a city peak hour.

            Hands above a page
            like mosquitoes.

Domestic

The one I love talks a lot
but it's often nonsense.

In some odd variety of dementia
she calls the door a bed.
Kitchen becomes laundry she
can never match names —
even amongst the family.

My lover does the unpleasant household chores
in return for massages.
Takes advantage of my disorganisation,
formal negotiations as she
swaps the filthy bathroom for
full body & ankle.

Whenever my lover gets involved in something
she forgets to breathe. Making love
this woman can alight on an interesting bit &
settle down.   But breathe!
There is either full silence
or if the lungs are full
air escapes in small, noisy
wheezes for what seems minutes.
Eventually some trigger clicks
& air comes in with great Labrador gulps.
Sex with my lover can be annoying.

She picks clothes on the basis
of colour & price.
Colour per kilo per dollar she
plods the shops... bag-lady brain
in old sneakers & last year's designer jeans

bought last week from grace bros.
Her war games are fought on mastercard.
The strategy sights targets: levi, faberge.

My lover keeps records obsessively, collates
a list of my failings & gives it to me
like a dead pet in xmas wrapping.

Okay, these faults are really mine, I
scratch out my name from this list & write
'my lover'.

She punches me once.
I look out the window & stop breathing

because our fights are always interesting.

Under the Weather

Fresh out of the shower
you sit down opposite & I wonder
at the one brazen drop, that runaway
tearaway bead sneaks down your cheek —
meets co-conspirators at the ear lobe
        abseils to the slowly rising nipple
            then joyously plummets
to the cheery springs of pubic hair.

You don't understand the cause of my wonder
but that's okay because we've been like this
beyond count, sometimes   beyond interest,
but we always return to this certainty of flesh.

I follow the path of those drops like their lowliest acolyte;
my tongue repeats their paths of reverence.

Hand shades in broadest strokes,
moves in to fine point/
the detailing of arousal.

You always say this is a dance,
demanded rhythms beyond timing.
Seek deepest resonance
where the music itself moves with you.

But to me we are painting —
the coax of colour from
beneath the white canvas of our skin.

My hands move hard, avoid the tender points
but nudge flesh towards those centres
as if your whole body congregates.

Your hands lap lightly
like a bay-protected tide.
You reach down & surprise us both
(because in these things we can all
be at the edges of extremity). A few words
& you come out to greet these fingers. I
come in as if some boulder easing into earth.

We seek the rhythms of your dance. Blood rushes north,
rushes south. My thumb
grinds nipple to fine ochre/   you are so intent

& have come, then try to come again but I miss cues
(as usual, imagination beats the art) —
have to wind down
to a calm, so calm that lakes are left looking
strung out & shabby/
      stillness poured from a distillation of afternoon sun/
           a book waiting in its store — gilt, ink & resin.

We sense a rhythm in the distance
as though initially it has nothing do with us:
something in the flat downstairs even
a movement deep in the crust.
Both concentrate,
try to find a point where it meets & seconds us.

It does.
This pulse is neither smooth, nor subtle.
You can't call it any relative
of waltz or bossa nova.
This is a storm.

Your hands are busy again,
a finger slips in
stirs frenzy in the spine.
Then you
then me. I lie on you.
Like moon-teased water you rise again from time to time —
those aftershocks you love.
Just... yes...
we move & are still simultaneous.

Just like this.

Hang On To Your Love

A certain kind of person
knows the words
fineprint perimeters
of romance,
desire.

But most love poems
just talk about the sensitive
& backlit prettiness
of the writer's own eyes —
internal fusion.

Few actually say that much about the other
bar nipple calling,
mouth's deep undertow/
the tug of all limbs.

She moves away to the other room
dances to Sade, sequestered.
Her time.

Maybe reciprocated
never shared.
Love is your own.

Can you truly love
& know all the other parts?

Last week it came from pain
bled trust.
He's unsure whether she moves then
or simply lets the music
clean. Sedate.

His gelled soot /wavy
develops a vagina-shaped bald spot that
makes no one fascinated or fond.
Enough drink, she thinks.

Her candlelit vulnerability
becomes a behavioural problem.

Must the name be Love?
By the treaties of clock & bridle
it is brittle
designed to go.
Dug up before a new season's planting.
Attacked by insects,
or rotted in the rain.

Can one aspire
to something deeper?
A house with its decades —
the knowledge of crooked doors
unhealed cracks
& fade of a north-facing winter porch.

From outside the closed door
the music all sounds
exactly the same.

Birthed

A couple are confounded beneath
fronds of surgical light, ruthless LED.
Making this minute island.
Nurses & the obstetrician wait busily as the father-to-be
surreptitiously sucks the nitrous oxide.

She is shipwrecked despite
the plans & training   push   breathe   breathe
Get this fucking thing out of me &
not a ripple of response from anyone   except
the partner who dabs at her brow with a damp cloth
as though he's tamping down grassfires
on this atoll's interior.

Lapping the shores
are the heartwaves of two beings,   mother & foetus.
Statistical narratives are duly noted down
by the clerical energies of Medicine.
18 hours & counting.
The indignity of miracles, the atrocity.
There's flurry, then cries
full of need & living.
A new small life
on this burnt summer's day.
Lorikeets lift from the palms outside as
here the deepest compact is born,
a covenant.

Both parents worry for the world
but feel sure there'll be space yet
for this tiny, mighty voice.

Tossed

This salad just as
our family life
contains ingredients one of us may not like.

In fact
one is bound
to notice garlic, capsicum & broccoli —
focus of strong opinions.

But
like our family life
collectively it tastes great

& will probably be good for us.

That's Ennn Tertainment

At the Maul we haul/crawl through bargins
till it's almost twelve
& the dear kiddies drag parents to the stage.
Time to rage.

Pop + flourish,
the smiles are wide enough that
engineers could lay
four lanes without blasting.

Before the real star,
BOG THE DOG arrives (in woofmobile),
a magician with four names & a tuxedo existences
this rabbit, his
loverly assistant is Tina /
         with training may eventually
         earn a surname.

Boomp boomp boomp
a plasticine bass line as
dancers' legs lift like mackerel in trawling nets   **this**
is school holiday entertainment &
the kids can join in, seventy
bopping bobbed heads in
enthusiastic mimicry of on-stage
knee-munching routines.

         Fun is replaced by intensity —
prize time arrives.
Stern lips call attention to their owners/
hands tensed like mousetraps to
snap a treasure.

I sit & plan tactics for
the forthcoming negotiations
(mcdonalds V Mexican).

One finale for the herd
then an inexplicable
sort of peace

penned in a forest of parents clutching k-mart bags
like rain heavy leaves.

◉

Out & About

Hand in hand
my pre-teen daughter & I move around
the sleepy Australian roar of her first demo.
She's quiet, busy eyes/ that
student over there on all fours
shirtless gold like
a day warming up.

The polite folk in marshal vests comb through
fingers brush this hairy head of belief.
Pulse of drums, breath comes in
as the crowd shifts &
ligaments of banners join muscle to bone...
We are a lumpy, lazy
varmint in the streets.

Green Left, Resistance
akubra & nike
joined for the first time
by a girl teasing out the
way of waves & wars —
teeth of ideas.

Speeches go on   words
an accompaniment to sunshine & city park fountain.

Then like galahs the flock rises to the beat
Racism OUT.
Cars fly past with a wave or complaint.
Ears are busy as always
but we are all naked here functionally —
subsumed to the conviction —

a mix of mechanical & vivacity
that naked always is.

Then I cry, grateful for the shades.

& my daughter, 12 years old is just
out of reach of everything —
but she stands
valued & vital
as any of those grey haranguers on that stage.
It's the best truths...

Healed & Hurt

I blame you & the island. There's an electronica,
champagne-strange tinnitus
that I wear like a lei. Feint complaint
from our hearts, all the uniforms are bleached.
We joke about hooking up a drip,
setting oxygen tanks beside
your breathless bed. King parrots attend to the gust
while afternoon storms then moonblaze
orbit that smile that we can make, that
has never been photographed, you
sometimes so serious doctor
who can both navigate the veins & be pulse.
Knave of the candle stick, have I ever been here before?
Yes, the familiars   mammal conflagration
plus our human excitability that builds or burns temples.
Forget about meaning or love, the scratch in the joints.
There's a kernel of a hearth. Who would have known
it was still there? We lose the crazy precision
breathless scission
of gasped words, *yes*
there a touch
our tongues dance they wear laughs,
forgotten eloquence...

are we *deduded*, maybe
langing in languor between kisses?
Will we eat, remember sleep? Mother, smother
or slather we experiment
& sweetly dement. This is it, this day at least...
the fires of your intelligence
when I am being stupid.
Wounds are sealed with diligent empathy. I am humbled
beneath your poems & palms.

Slipshod eucalypts clothe sky,
bestride the oblivious, the loveliness.
Shy around lemons & fingerlimes
we ripen.

Requiem for a Squid

A solitary pelican cut the moon
reflected on the implacable still
of the Hawkesbury River.
Atrociously white,
that glide on the surface with barely a ripple.

Perhaps this scratch of night
was peace for us,
hand in hand on the jetty.
We'd already shed unnecessary words.

But for the bird it was lazy predation.
Does each moment carry
these opposing aspects?
Like estuarine erosion
does death & catastrophe seep
into all our lives' careful abutments?

A dive, the pouch writhed with its catch —
some kind of answer.

Dearly Demented at the Sundowner Nursing Home

1. Birthday day

Pollock lipstick
vagabond slippers, the snug imprisonment of tracksuits
blotched with 11:30 soft-diet lunch.

Begin to hope the progress
behind pharmacological ramparts.
The real medicine is touch
all other expertise unnecessary.

I am now a fixture here
the nurses chat at visits, even read my books
between wiping bums &
perennially guiding Tommy back to bed.
Clinical notes recorded on the verge —
chasms of new molecules,
pneumonic harmonica & missing limbs.
I sing along at this birthday party
when everybody else thinks it's theirs.
Cordial & cake fly like confetti
slow motion kindergarten.
There's the bazaar worth of plots afoot
scheming over nullity
stolen wedding rings
or dentures. Buccaneers are aloft
in the rigging of their wheelchairs/
aluminium walking-frames glint dangerously
in a gatecrashed refulgence that
cranks gaiety to a cackled fever.

2. Pick Me Up

Each visitor is like a death, still hanging on
rusted to every mother as she's caught
keening into where.

The constant spatter of TVs —
worlds come in to seduce away facts
that have still clung on
(steel hooks in the cerebellum).
Always music somewhere
cassette recordings of pianos built with
ceramic tiles instead of strings
Underneath the Arches
We'll Meet Again
(& just once My Generation sent a ripple of anxiety
through attendant babyboomers).
The heart patch of stone nursed,
mouths open like day
eyes turn tail in remembrance
for this week's Deeply Departed.

3. Kind Regards

My mother is "such a lady"
& they love her in the way
of driftwood, stars & paper cuts.
The dependable burn of cigarettes,
flags of clarity & void, alternate horrors each
in separate ways. Time as soil erosion.
Some kind of word in a sleeping night.
Commonwealth Care Standards
alongside the guilt of children.

All is managed
yet there's a kind of anarchy,
painted over every three months then
marked on coloured charts.

Families play a hackneyed role —
their fret, love
& secret wishings.
It washes over staff who've seen it all before.
There are always better,
always worse actors for these parts.
It's a morality play
written in DNA
'cause Mum's dementia
will probably be our inheritance.
Partners & doctors monitor afternoon snores,
measure our decline.

4. Lost Post

This is some kind of harvest
old flesh on brittle bones
grey wheat above
episodic eyes.
Who says death is better?
Most of us
(today: tinned salmon in a weak tomato sauce).
Usually not the residents
encrusted
sometimes even the mad, tender collegiality
of senescent love affairs —
even though she calls him
by another name & his face
is netted alongside unrelated memories.

In the sound of the sun,
every day is new.
Ambulances arrive
more regularly than friends —
there's the thrill of the ride
beneath panic, balms
& the not-so-silent rite of agony.

These veterans wear their ribbons of scars...
the Battle of Afternoon Tea.
Pain management.
Come half past five
That Bloody Olga nods off,
above *Deal or No Deal*
an outpost of transcendence.

The Bed

His last word was *poetry*.

By then the lot was shutting down
just a few jittered pumps.
He was an immobile, breathless bird. Plucked. Flensed.

An unplanned consciousness
(they manage death there with a considerate rigour)
& that word
infiltrated
as precipitation seeks out the tiniest lacuna in shelter.

The voice had no scope left
for inflection or those other contexts
like the grammar of promiscuous hands.

It could have been a promise;
postcard back to his
tribe of the living.

Maybe a plea — him strung with pain
& cottonwool chains of morphia.
But this treatment he demanded...
none to give.
Like always, it's a puzzle for a fraud —
some suspicious brown bottle
from a frayed, nomadic carnival.
Hungers let this word
stretch across words.

Some kind of battle cry?
Victory was impossible
yet warriors still rallied,

the hoplite loosed his fiercest call —
a primal boom.

Perhaps this was the summary
dropped down to those two who were present.
(audience size typical for our artform).
Just as us all, his hands had
navigated through bad rhymes
reining in a terrier context
as it raced down new streets
digging frantically in loam
for just a whiff of image.
These flimsy bridges were all we had,
the chasms of stanza break.
Poverty that left us all
sometimes desiccated & silent.

Just possibly
it was a prayer.
Yes, this word can be so
when all the rest
are drab suburban grids.
Our scabbed, hard works stand out
when no more remains.
This spirit, the guts
are blessed towers.

He was weak...
a poacher with one last, huge spoken catch
wriggling in his hands. But no one took it back,
it had become his
entitled by the price of breath,
hod-hours of bared ribs.

His poetry was a sung
shred of ligament.
Just as the body abandoned food, then water
all the diversions, flounce & tune-work
were jagged down at this level —
elemental as pulse
in a tight, marginal being.
Sometimes an implacable poem comes at you like death.
As often the piece never works
until you take it under the lake,
one last chance.

Next day I held him
but he'd taken all the art
that February had to offer.
It was secreted in his tumulus
a chariot   the helmet   the jewels.

A year later, near Long Point in this choired winter,
I see a rock face that is visibly crumbling
to an indolent apricot dust.
Its feet stumble in the detritus of itself.
I take up a desultory shard
& write *poetry* on that surface in tiny,
surprisingly collected strokes.
Imagine it will soon corrode away
while being seen by very few.
Among the readers
there will be confusion, distaste

but perhaps just a touch of awe
from one or two who wander
with a need   & spare time to impale
on the teeth of four sapling eucalypts
staking out vacated earth.

Landed

The wilds are unmarketable
thereby valueless?

Veldt

We bring death & our lawns.
Savannah sacks across the seas
dressed as plenty & called colonisation.
Sharpshooters, architects — meaningless,
salmon in shoes. Pitter patter is the matter.

Native grasses are superseded
tarmac cravat
buck-formal pretend
it's not just a phase.
The impulses of our darker part trail behind
tails tucked — a false concession
all drool with clarity,
lap at the leaving life.
What about our art?
It is just another flame.
We lope towards the wreckage.
Grass half full,
we always

choose to stay.

Jerusalem Track

The smoke has become
another season.

An element.

It collects around the trees, makes
their leaves seem weighted, a curve
in that trunk suggests recoil but
this place is just
doing the business as I walk through a forest
that anticipates the imminent
feast of fire under a chanting mat of cicadas.

Elsewhere flames explode on touch
rich eucalypt oils,
minute white flowers lost in a sunburst.

Will my season end so
smudged & furious? Perhaps
there is no alternative
— summers never surrender —
it's always declared war against heat
by an undermining wind as the world turns over
to warm its other half.

I write this as I sit
on an outcrop looking down at the Hawkesbury,
watch the younger man climb the slope
(so much energy,
spraying uselessly).

Turn see an aged man behind,
not embarrassed to be caught in his thoughts over me.

So we too are seasons.

We too are smoke. Free & inevitable.

Hidden Valley

Just beneath the pool's surface,
slipping like a syringe
beneath the sun-struck dermis,
there is a teal crystal vibrancy.

My clumsy hairy hands rest there
supplicants, stunned
by a spun grace.

High above on scaffolds
teams work with tarpaulins,
wrapping the sun
for a subtler illumination.
At the ridge top, tour buses kneel/
corrugated iron sheds stop rusting
to better hear the harmonies.

Fingerlings pass like eras,
water weeds belly dance — courtesans
to the smaller, vastly potent
sister of light.

A day to her honour, this green brilliance her church,
my bent shoulders her rough prothesis.

Meaning is here
but at the periphery
like an odd uncle at a kid's party. Other,
brighter energies steal the show.
The world works wonders.

Trail

Soprano birdcall dance around the bass
line of freeway traffic just beyond this
confluence of trees.

Pass a *memorial* boulder, the insufferable subtlety of tiny
wildflowers on a mat of olive drab.

Down to the river, mud flats.
Lizards lurk in crevice,
two crows argue in the trees like
a drunk couple at a wedding
too long past their own.

Three opalescent fish dart between the blunt grace of
a floating garbage (heavy duty) bag.

German tourists happily stomp by, a group
so self-contained that the scenery begins to look like
the portable part of this tableau.

More stone, more nature.
That unusual man in a raincoat hides
behind a hundred-year-old blackbutt.
Fifteen feet above, an endangered species sits —
entirely unaware of its star status.

> We trudge through this mad salad
> as my child talks philosophy, inspired
> by something in the air.

Flung Far South

In an accident of clear light
undressed leaves bend
to the fragile gleam of a breathless lake.

The forest floor steams,
basks in 12° — deep mind —
the sonar of birdcalls.

Mossy sheep are more like boulders — this place
where the football field has lichen instead of grass.

Where everyone drinks *Cascade Beer* —
by rain-rotted roads, bottles emptied/enduring — *Cascade*!
Beside waterfalls
& alongside elegant teardrops of granite
Cascade, Cascade
(& dead packets of *Horizon 30s*
near white-spotted scarlet toadstools).

Kangaroos — as they run away from intruders
one tends to see
only tail & arse, the landscape murmurs
to an accompaniment of drums.

Showers falter, shadows disperse, gouache sun. One moment.
Then kids desert their homes,
collapse of cupboarded play to
a chitter down the footpaths.
Canopy totters at the edge of our eyes
while an indifferent kookaburra
shakes shadow from its wing.
All work is display.

Roadstone

Strands of thylacine fur snagged
in the rush of rivers through turbine generators.
The past stands like a startled sheep
in the headlights of our journey.
All plans
generate heat.

When we are still   bacteria's rheumy eyes
sprout by cottonballs of inclemency.

Padded sky — needlepoint showers, yet another rainbow.
Churning topaz, delinquent Derwent River.
Our feet about an old-growth stand
waterlogged eucalypts give long spinal cracks — the forest moans.
Cloudstruck greens of southern rosellas rustle tree to tree
like couriers. Fresh winds thrash leaves — hyped, flighty.

A wallaby flops back into cover... surprised, distracted farce.
Two Tasmanian devils rumble under scrub,
ferns flung aside in rage.   The patina of green
beneath a wind-whisked lake.
Brown trout immobile,
pregnant opacity.
            Deep tincture of winter.
                Trees shiver in lichen rags.

At the end of the day there is no colour left.
Sun surrendered,
but shrugged as it did so.
Brothers ice & wane can have this ground.
Complexity is lost. Mists above a lake
are more lit than the sky. Shrubs, grass,
snow on a distant peak/   reduced to monotone.

I am still on the roadside, intent.
Beneath a scarred, ponderous moon
chorus from the taint of stars.

Riverina Weather Report

This is a catalogue of prayer
beneath the rooftop brawl of possums\ /
tossed ink Saturday night
with a searchlight moon engraved with curses
& growls of freight trains heading north.
I think about us.

Like the furry clash on tin
our choices are inescapable
each rimed with peril
with its roots in a loam of convenience.
This winter has lurched up
like half-dead livestock.
Rain is a miser's drip
of hope over odds. Our world is warming.

Will it happen for us
our new bridges of silence
the paddock gates we close, lock
with corroded chain
& hand-shaped latches?
We are promised some kind of haven
but without fodder.

To aspire to the life of smaller birds,
the gold clamour of wings as they flit amongst
smudged olive leaf & incandescent lilli pilli berries.
I will try again
on the next return. League's Club dinner
& three glasses of champagne.
The affirmation of our fingertips,
habit of our hearts.

Broken Hill

1. Coming Inside

Flags outside the Legion Club
are ricepaper.
Talk to them about the cool geography
of a won peace.
No rocks have it given freely
& the four Goths in this metal town
are working up a thirst.

Broken Hill wears its collar up.
Loiter beside breath, cutting the eye,
the skimp dump is an Uluru of mining waste.
You bend back your neck
scrape a taste.

2. Down Argent St

Lives dyed poverty & something stronger.
People here wear only
the nonsense they choose.
CHRISTMAS PAGEANT — the floats
from distance haulage, pasminco & community teams,
the *simply there* tools that hold a life together.
Flying guts & panadol white on flatbed — St John's Volunteers
but now no Goat Girl to mascot
the soccer team after all those years.
While here on the footpath — father, four kids stare astonished
at their woman's blasted fury —
come out of nowhere like a whirly, she
stood around too long, chose combustion over corrosion.

Quandong pies, mine bosses' lies,
history weighs.
Listen to the stories — from boxing, camel drover, fruit picking.
I know so little. A local points down, says
*Them ants **stop** massin' when it's gunna rain.* It may be a joke.

The range of front yards from satellite dish
in a handkerchief of desert
(hard as dole forms)
to imported tint bordering arduous lawn.
Then in a place
where the sweet are less displayed —
apricots splay under a fat peach sun.

Poets belong here… lead, zinc & silver
mined, then mined again
extracting from diminished grades.

3. Collecting the News

Way down in Adelaide
swimmer lost at sea
two bodies found wrapped in plastic by a dry riverbed.
Newsreader promises another fine day at *The Hill*
with an ecclesiastic certainty.

100k east, by Lake Menindee Sunset Strip holiday cottages
(improbable beach architecture, one lazy road)
pelicans water ski as
two mulga parrots argue in the shade.

Over iced Melbourne beer we talk about
Clydesdales wearing hard leather hats
strapped then lowered
for a nine-day shift by candlelight.

Generations of miners, warrior wives —
their babies swaddled in lead dust.
Unions built with bloodshot brick & sweating mortar

Arts Centre — Barkindji Auntie fills an order
oil on board, red —
we discuss useless doctors, bad knees.
That night men read their poems in shorts.

4. Metal

Down baseline, the carwash throws
water like loose change on the heads
of late model 4WDs.
Next door a tin house so fractured
so *movie* with rings of dead automobiles
left from each decade snared
from a scarred blue sky.

There is nothing as frugal as shade
up here on the rise
at Block 10.

Hemmed by horizons of spat stones,
dunes of debris
traffic buzzes idly
in mockery of itself.
A mineral town where earth is both
an easy touch & the Saturday night beating
when she *didn't do ANYTHING*.
Almost covert, words are done
from tree to tree, sips from a bottle.

Around the water tower
junk from men

seeps down the thirsts of ground below\\
light stuck grey of loose lost gneiss
heroic weeds & a red kangaroo.
Desert finches amongst the gumnuts.

Then at the peak — burnt wood, cut rock.
We see it all corrode as eyes are led away
down the Mundi Mundi Plains...
delicate dustflower whirlies
(true sky-scrapers) march
toward their own collapse, exhausted dancers
lunged to drink.

Distant hills are their own making
& will not engage recent unravelment.

Eyes dive in an improbable pond.
I leave the tired steel
of books & pen.

Our extremities always taper at crisp white screens.
Who is writing me?

5. Blood's Red Noise

By the verge — hit then harvested —
a tail-taken kangaroo.[1]
Highway 32's dead,
crash'n'carry.

Then, as you walk right out
beyond a desert town's bluster lawn & air-condition —
the squeeze of silence.

---

1 The best eating part of this animal is the tail, regularly harvested from
recent roadkill.

Your shoes crash land,
this macadam braid
on the dryland's thin skull.
One bird sounds like late-night TV
the breeze an argument in progress.

Empty gun air abrades a skin which no longer fits/
excavates the bladder.

Your clothes are a barbed wire fence
as fingers wriggle down towards the burrow.

You have mined the shrubs for moisture
built houses on remote hills of chance.

The sweaty truth there now is a need
to listen to oneself.

6. Then Someone Goes

Late arvo, the *Indian Pacific* grabs blue metal
rolls it like a cigarette. My trip − feet/bags/
preposterous brochures talk of destination & rules.
The woman alongside, her eyes are a seismic fault.
I am another one leaving
as lives ferment into lines.

Aeolus at the Mulga

The desert wind wears a blunt dust
cantankerous yap
lifts sheetmetal
from the deaths
of the snub-nosed Silverton buses all
cut like raw opal
pressed into a humiliating servitude
windbreaks for camels.
Punctuation of eagles
affixed on air.
The land is your lungs
but flies have retired as the gale wails.
Ants flummox
by vertebrae of quartz
garnet veined.
Beneath this lee
my eyes are lost. This wind is a tide
only bones bask
on gasping sand — that 'roo spine
sits prissy, 90° against
the perimeters of stone.
A huff of emus
disperse like seeds as I approach.
This is a vacated day
feet crash on pepper.
We have built much
the skipsy genes that jitter
past our hands.
Falter — this adamance shuts the mouth

comes over, spits
that coming shine we smelt from rocks.
Death by a purpose
still destiny to bend
the nuisance of new sense.
Only dry scat is left on the 100km mat.
Concession is prayer
excoriation,
we make brushes.
God could be a wind
& heaven is a spot...
safely away from its hands.

Fremantle

Money makes money, it breeds.
New Carthages arise to be wrecked.

I stopped & listened
when a crow dropped pine needles on my head
in this *historical* town.

The complaint of Whadjuk middens...
built across centuries,
buried by convict labourers
salted by wharfie sweat
papered over with banknotes.

By a modest puddle
in a public park
I recognise we have to work our failures
as hard as our wins.

I tried to sow outrage
but under this sun nothing takes.
More needles drop on me,
on the busyness... Freo's
heritos, archeos, ecos, physios & psychos.
This town is so me.

Arms open down on the beach, tour buses yawn
& dinner plates clap heartily from the sidelines.

Burnt Rubber at the Dead Zone

Elena has a new art, her paintbrush
this silver *Kawasaki Big Ninja, ZZR-1100,*
plus a radiation detector.

Woman of speed & silence,
technology beyond fingers, a stretched drum-skin of
void & straw where the
Monkey Law of Curiosity is written in nettles.

She rides through Chernobyl taking photos —
the Luminous Law of Poke.
Only snow promises "reconciliation".

A few declining shards of occupation, even tour guides.
But visitors cannot stay —
canned by quiet, the innate dissonance
of human clutter without the tribe…
well-fed eyes skitter,
shoulder muscles clench beside placards
for the 1986 Mayday Parade
Party of Lenin leads us to the Triumph of Communism.
Magazines unread, *Fish & Hunt.*
Kindergarten excursions are postponed
for 30 generations.

"Chernobyl" means wormwood[1] &
is an iridescent palette. This woman passes
corroded nidus of tanks, Sikorski bones. My own

---

1 "And the name of the star is called Wormwood: and the third part of the
waters became wormwood; and many men died of the waters, because they
were made bitter." (Rev. 8:10, 11)

daughter was born that week when the world leaked,
an alp of news alongside slow, implacable
contractions as we watched
Nightmare on Elm St, then *Cheers*.

A hoar of antiquity in the toss of their manes
Prejevalsky Horses shave grasslands,
this new age of life —
roses go the way
of any managed thing.
A patch of armistice as
confident wolves ignore the scent of dead farmyards.
Wild boar multiply, move into simple wooden huts that
drink radiation but refuse to desert
their concord of shelter.

The Ferris ("Devil's") Wheel will not turn.
Washing, 20 years untouched, still on the line.
Vovik + Tanya = love (maybe still/
600 miles away & them nervously with new children
waiting for the taint).

Elena reassures us
that bitumen protects,
doses at their lowest in the centre of roads.
No one is surprised by this,
enduring haven of we brutes that ate.
Is this the last human ecology?
Roars of our engines, the septic gasp.
Opal eyes peering from tarmacadam coats.

Pointy End

It sees that sky
this big fat city
& of course has to poke it.

They pave over everything
even the air holes.

Build sharp, don't stop
only dare to ponder
when there is an auction for naming rights
to that shed previously called heaven.

I can see the light, just.
In summer there's the appearance of life
but in the hard winter we people
are smears, shivering afterthoughts.
Connected only by the viruses we share.

Mine the Gap

1. London Ticket

Burnin' & Luton.
Double deckers, (grumbled thrum) they outnumber
furtively immobile cars that stand out like
bermuda shorts as this simmered commute falls in a line.

Shy eyes on the opposite seat.
Everyone's talking the new
hoodie happy slap, kid in school uniform —
some geezer   deep asleep on the #56
POW! Open handed & all a
mobile uplink, web pages showing
right lippy bitches their struck-up faces
as the whack cracks.
You see those hoodies wif phone man me
eever run or fight back no regrets
a Happy Kicking from me man
for this is RIGHT OUT OF ORDER.

London, tattooed with arrival —
trains like duressed armour, devastating when failed.
Long-distance buses are a sort of death
every bodily function closes down in
an odoriferous, slumped shuffle.
Dyke against wood, episodic rose.
Wavelets of waste, the empty corpse in equality.
British steam power. Empire
scars & bloody expertise.

2. Rush

He said with a tired smile,
jazz stubble & vagrant eyelids
Doen be worried mon, it happen oorll dee time.
This city of paperwork & death/
medieval towers stacked with ragged memos
'till new glass grows
to shroud our words. Tourists graze
around spat & polished ramparts.
Kinder vanity, wild gravy.
The acupuncture of the End.

National security, social security.
The English value politeness, chains.

This busy place
a new salad age
where mortgages are monarchs.
I revel in its clash,
both archaic & effervescent.
She calls him by the window
to bed.

Knuckled pink/mauve
10-year-old Hackney "witch" all smashed.
Her bones were kindling.

Press Curl, Gel Twist, Cut-tong, Afro Kinky-curl ££SAVE££.
300 African kids, just missing...
filing errors, lost in scree.
Dykes — great earthen ramparts set against a lamp,
daft collegiality of howl.

Scumshite!

Prissy history. The deep poison rests
in the 4th ventricle of the bladder, holding back,
left behind & wrecking the place.

I think as a pop star
there'll be a lot of arse-shaking to be done…

Fear nothing & so much
reading Rupert Murdoch
STRIPPER LIQUIDISED FLATMATE IN BLENDER.

3. Rubble in the Jungle

Her patron saint of queues colours each pavement
dead barley brown, disembowelled drear.
Concrete harp of clarity in pain,
the profane miasma of Westminster Abbey —
power & gold leaf smother
all that is spiritual or real.
Dyke against a shroud.

Rowboats, Romulans,
Roman rubble & raconteurs.
Lonely windows will not open.
Everything important wins. Dyke against different skin,
sanctified suicide snagged on a barb. Plots of Energy.

At the Karl Marx Memorial Library
silverfish live in equality & plenty.
Blair's Britain paid for its
shiny new door & security intercom.

Here's the homeless cadge
a clog on one foot, trainer on the other... under the bridge
London *came into some money*
200 years ago. Jacina just wants some.

4. Grass

Above the stuffy, noisy avarice
all nature here is construct.
Every hill is a castrated mountain but
such landscape work with hoe & grader
is perhaps the greatest English art

Pretty Park[1] those social engineers knew
the dumb seduction of colour & leaf.
Just as planned, our pace falters —
peace within pause
fret frenzy is stifled into
the regency of eyes,
gazebo placebo.
On Hampstead Heath
doolally petals borrow wind,
moussed grass bows before the flattery of mowers.
Where's your stick? The setter looks
momentarily bereft
then backtracks, retrieves.
This moment is flawless for every animal present.

Breeze lullabies fields of wildflowers...
if you hanker for angst
this is a kind of dell-hell,
Victorian stone bridge over

---

1 IMO Kevin Coyne

what even ducks call a drain.
Service through decay.
Solitude complete
(even though another path
is just feet away). *Catch me is u can.*

5. Anorak at SW4

Despite the gold
the two of us, back again…
maid fret & green light balloons.
Former homes, but like Tube trains on different lines
connection is a concept only —
here you can lose yourself
forget any chance
of your name called across traffic.
National Poetry Centre — what noise does a poem make
if it falls in a forest of people?
Concrete harp of mind, colourslip.

Amidst immobility, traffic lights flicker like fans;
the leaking gravel rash of carmine paint.
Just by Holy Trinity I see Marina —
our accidental collusion of tint
32 years ago in the nearby squat.
She used to be famous. My history there,
the astonished not-quite new man.

6. Breath

HOTTEST MAY DAY IN 50 YEARS
Buses, befuddled to a standstill… boiled dementia.
Swinging into the #88, he's an assertive dishevelment
I dinna like these days very much —
if it keeps up oy'll be back to Scotland!
Pneumonic high, a viscous momentary grab.

Hyper new mothers swap attitude
bikini tops sharp against Black torsos.
Lambeth Paddling Pool slowly fills with water.
As a tantara of ravens drink
plopped down by the valve
one stolid 3-year-old plays with a bucket,
wavelets of primary happiness, a concrete hand of solace.
Clapham Common Old Town sheds
as I cry.
She calls me by my decade.
This place that birthed so much
while it side-tracked simultaneous. Born & baffled.
Where's Wicksy?
           Back in London/Sydney.
None of this seems right
amidst a slapstick sunshine.
Half a lifetime seems like three.
Embittered brick impassive slate
White walking-cane windows,
some fallen right out in
one of the last squatting communities in London
still with its ageing musicians, young poor.
Just as we had planned back then around coal fires &
nicotine-rich spliffs (crumbs of Lebanon)
— amidst the ruins of No.16
an unauthorised park defies the glare.

This man walks in his
good life, will & a few
belongings, chasms of money
waves of abandon(ment).
Fetters of Energy.
No gallery of the end.
Vines have eaten the backyard
of my old home.

7. Flight

The day after is a city heaving...
relief, stress or asthma?
That heat back again
like a remembered fight amongst friends,
some greenstick honeymoon gone wrong.
Gritty wind bullies up from Spain
frail glass, doors, the leaves
rattled, busy in the oak.
Her behaviour was so lewd... I was shoct.

My last bus goes to Angel, #38, still a 50s growler
the official red of all once run
for & by the People. Almost the lot is owned now,
even houses.

Above the rain, there is more colour
the congress of fort
(a martial state on benefits).
It's hair art, stuffed foxes
betting shops   a crashed-realm bingo hall.
Castles & churches are tethered lions —
the only things caught are passing eyes
while the real London is toasted
on the Turkish café's charcoal griddle.
It's a disability parade, some sort of vibrancy,
the wrecking ball
above all   a gurgle of paintpeeled downpipes
playing so many anthems
for us all alive somehow,
for this rustle in the world burrow.

Kozhikode

1. Eagles

The friendly attendants lead me to my cage.
I have air, water & newspaper lining the base.
Windows struggle with the light.

Call from my comfortable containment to the raptors
above a car storage lot next door — those sedans all new with
their wipers pulled out from the windscreens
like the antennae of snoozing cockroaches.

There's a hint of ant nest
out on Mavoor Rd.
A bit of beetle in the stalls selling phone accessories.

Eagles here hardly ever seem to land...
this weave of air they inhabit
while commerce crawls & crunches below.
Pomegranates tumble towards earth.
Spice films all surfaces.

The city is the birds' business too
though I can't imagine what they eat
or where their roosting hides.

Earthbound in a mix of compassion & abuse
busy with necessities & dreams,
our scuttle lacks any sense of grace.
How did people like us
build or banish all *this*
with these flightless hands?

2. As We Speak

Anaya, this tiny woman sharing the festival car
usually has security 24/7.
She has a great sense of humour.

While academics worry they are being ignored
her campaign against sex slavery
has seen eight assassination attempts.

Mavoor Rd wears commerce.
Three cars behind, an "official" Toyota seems
to own all placidity available in this heat.

She has a remarkable set of numbers,
one could tally the collective
weight of guilt. I mostly just listen.

There are etiquettes, expectations. Of course power, delusion
& rape underpins much. Outside the shelters of Culture
her voice has been an annoying wind across the sub-continent.

One Bedia patriarch has declared
her campaign will enslave *his* girls in worthless marriage.
Sons must now do menial labour.

The status quo is no temple, it's a veil.
Sometimes there are arguments it's a load-bearing wall,
necessary obscenity for institutional process.

Occasionally landlord gods are named as co-defendants.
They sneer at feeble courthouses
put up without remedies or insight.

Early bed for her as there's a 6am flight to Delhi.
Men headline that seminar
& she has a strict 10min allocation.

In the Green Room, Mary complains she's got
so little left to write about.

Chengdu – After the Festival

Certainty & knowledge are not compatible.
This city both misses
& overtakes the point.

The way forward is a brighter light.
We are asked
to mistake the glare for truth.

One's eye avoids the cracks
but I am told there is a fine script there too.
Even the trees wear a progressive concrete.

I have been shown a future
though thankfully children here still fidget
& pick their noses.

We are all done by Sunday afternoon,
tables cleared, rooms repolished.
Those with destinations are despatched.

Down in the backstreets
a sweeper's bin is full.
She sleeps in the amnesty of shade.

Her split-bamboo broom preens.
José thinks the air is gasping,
I think it sighs.

By the important building
a sentry, so straight
could be plaster.

Except now he yawns.
I think he dreams
of riverbanks.

Dogs discard their leashes.
There is talk of love again
& a gwailou's tears are preposterous.

Hopeland LA

Pay the money, ride
'till judgement day
these early breakfast eggs sprawl beneath
a dawn-light beacon of bacon as
the racked-toast sits planted like palms.

DRUGSTORE, barn sized, never shut. Its aisles/
pain relief, socks & deck chairs.
PINK PUSSYCAT   blinks quietly,
a building knitting.
The smoky patois
of Harry in the Downtown Sports Bar.
Alcohollywood   this is world culture.

Wandering hopers, wannabees swarm in the smog.
Front yards are infested with "writers"; those
chitinous predators with their lousy lines.
Along the Hollywood Walk of Fame
"actors" drop their cigarettes.

It's Beginning to Look a Lot Like Christmas.
Torn lottery tickets
pass for snow, this is March.
That manic crooner outside the metro
has too much ice in his blood
& too little coin in his Santa hat.
Reindeers join the other fawns on Sunset.

A relentless midday —
"Girls just wanna have FUNdamental rights"
placard in the picket outside
24HR NUDE North Hollywood "Pay & we'll play".

A few hundred dance & drum down by the tideline,
a thirty-minute tribe while
police SUVs sift sand in their talons.
VENICE BEACH FREAK SHOW opens
as the sun collapses into its salty bath —
washing off that air.

$40 gets you a medical marijuana assessment,
the queues outside are disturbingly flaccid.
Roller blades rust like a season,
one successful applicant turns towards the sea.

Glare abandons the city
as does so much else.
Newly born each evening like the city's
Santa Ana wind racing from the desert.
This divorced, aging metropolis
is just another brittle celebrity.

Railway Town

Where I grew up there was respect for the uniform.
No one ever killed in them. Armed with timetables
the wise station men & women handled the public
like important post, parcels of love.

On the 2nd floor of the 19th century schoolhouse
serious career advisors charted my promotion...
Station Master if I only *applied myself.*
Snuck off for a smoke out the back
while they enthused lamely to recidivist Timmy
on the life of a shunter.
Were our limitations already infused
into our stubbled DNA?

This is a cogent universe.
In the goods yard,
on an icy nightshift in Outer Junction
my older brother James lost his right arm.
They reassigned him to Correspondence —
one-handed, two-finger typed missives
trickled into the mail chutes for the next 40 years.

Our local university eschewed anything practical
so I graduated with a nuanced world view
alongside no prospects beyond the Transit Recruitment Office
where I professed a love for signal boxes
& got groped by a senile physician — the "physical".

My parents cried at the ceremony
when I was awarded braided epaulettes.
That gold crown badge on my midnight peak cap
shone like a quietly proud moon.
Anywhere in the world

a fellow railworker will give you shelter.
This community of Process,
engraved conclusions,
nothing I've seen elsewhere can compare.

All my life has been ordered.
I knew cars never made sense.
Successive governments & technology
were just rustles in the trees.
Lines became electrified, then duplicated.
The Rail Way is the answer.

My grandchildren are strangers
living far away in computers
but I won the 2014 Station Garden Competition.

Bloom

Suburbs now have their community gardens.
Husbands buried there
turn the pages of books abandoned
because the heroine fretted too much
to actually *do*.

This ambition to compost sees mounds
of Key Performance Indicators,
municipal fantasies in leisure suits,
child custody papers, electricity bills...
all the rubbish
that makes Australian Progress.

Flowers that bother to turn up
have abandoned their happy-face.
Willows whinge as magpies singe the cyclists.
Fertilise is the chorus, a sentence.

Babies in rusted enclosures
plot revolution as they always have.
Mummies sip the gin
to let themselves out
to let themselves in.

This isn't hell, there's
methane rather than sulphur
& our local sun has been ordered to shine without
meal breaks or recompense.
Another grandparent is complaining,
counts on being ignored —
part of her perpetual motion machine.

This project called putrescence
is the whole   the last point.
It will take a lifetime,   the only way out, no parole
so scratch on the walls of sky
those years passed, those few remaining.

The Sydney Problem

Doesn't matter what you eat when
what you eat doesn't matter.
The Grapes of Sloth
squelch.

By the shore — washed up teeth of pianos.
Our maps of art are bereft, the city is saved from
historical clutters that we
(exactly three of us) have fought to preserve.

The sun covets pink hotels. Inside the last bestial roar
comes from aircon. But wait for it, no worries.
If the books are written I will have a hat.
Writings have become as obsolete as atlases —
though remnant beauties grow from cuttings
in a pot rich with blood'n'bone but

on Sundays all are bought by Plenty, this
city with its polished shells, the driftwood
desolation that is a kind of sensuality.
Nothing "postal", Trinket Town will
outlive all our complaints.

This miraculous club
disturbed by 658 *lesser* suburbs they
hang around like groupies,
an embarrassment.

Another superb day, trees like oiled slaves
weave their shade about our fret. You can't stay mad when
you're never hungry. My trial before a barbeque bench
is over in minutes... all the witnesses would rather drink.

Guitar riffs from the ridge,
blowsy sails loll about the reef.
Another bottle, another war elsewhere...
all generals should become wedding planners so
our remaining factories can just make cakes.

Skin, the last art. Leave those tongues
for pleasure. Our delusions debride,
that pus we call worry. Even storms are just sound effect,
the devil's in the dovetail
would anyone *really* change this?
Sydney summer says it all, 3D Bose sound.

Those few dissidents left caught a train home
to fill out job applications.

Water Ways

Invest in bricks & water.

Two Ghosts & the Diesel Crow-choir

Black highway, reflective
"1" & the moon exchanged stares
across truckless distances of space.

Me — four hours standing, just past the bridge
dropped off
from a country town lust adventure, getting late
hitching south back
to the Old Big Smoke.

Past 11, past 12.
North coast cold rose up as if
the river below shed a frozen skin/
like it was throwing out a net of itself
to catch a night-stunned world.

& out of *that* mist came two women.

I'd been dancing on the spot, singing to an emptiness
in that free solitude.
Staying warm too,
part of a truth.

Straight dissection of road
up to the bridge. The following dip
had become a reprehensible welcome mat.
No traffic for almost 30 minutes &
no nibble for hours not
even a hesitation before the gush of passing air,
eruption of roadstone.

Then these two
distinct beneath moonlight, one

in a long dress, other in jeans they
ambled across the bridge, occasionally leant into touch
as they shared secrets, drunken bump suggesting
history & trust.

There was an unease to the picture, as
though the road was suddenly crowded, some
blueprint ignored to be three people
lingering in this isolation & time.

Putting down the mild hysteria of waiting
I called out welcome, moved towards them.

In the distance
a turpentine smudge of light grew
to the conflagration of hibeam
& the diesel crow-choir wailed
as a truck became a cannon
& the valley was scoured in panicked shadow.

Revealing an empty bridge.

Five times those women walked —
not once made it past that long concrete-bone bridge
before vanishing under headlights.

Did they have a story?
Bodies that also never passed this creek,
perhaps one night flesh too was pierced by light
as the formwork pavement gave way to weeds & sand
on this bitter highway.

How much pain to affix them to the tarmac
beyond even life?
Did they hear me call out,

consider this man with his bag edging closer
or was all this entirely locked within themselves,
an audience meaning nothing?

I jumped, a flea through the hours.
Trapped
between these repeating visions
& the echoes of earlier gropings at the local cemetery,
the contact for both so
hungrily sought &
the provision in the end of no sustenance.
We are wrapped in urges, impassable moments
repeated across time.

Still the night-tinted waves of grass
one beaten gum & moon.
Heartfelt
on asphalt   around 5 a salesman pulled up.
I had a story to tell & told it hungrily;
as though this needed to be out,
quickly reduced to
words & the artificial normality of shared commentary.

He was called Bob, I think, suggested coffee at a diner...
barely 6 kilometres
the woman there serving no nonsense
as the thick brewed coal on dawn formica-morning did it all.

Moon-ridden,
fragments of me were still waiting
for those thieving headlights.

Shaky hands & swollen oyster eyes
reached back again
to the bridge,

to the endless wander of two women
caught forever on a river's raw hook.

Moon

I was thinking then
that no one can write any more
about rivers & full moons.
They are themselves complete statements,
an accretion of still.

But there was a moon last night
above the bleeding mist —
possum caught in porch light
her eyes just as round, febrile.
Across the valley, Wagga shot its lights
like coughed up sparks above a conflagration.
The speed sign had its shadow
(moonshadow — a boiled-chicken word, abruptly understood)
& I shivered, moving on
my feet on blue metal, grounded in civilisation.

Then yes, next day
the Murrumbidgee is muttering
as "capital improvements" tweak her shore.
Three teenagers at the "beach"
two shopping carts in the shallows
like burrs on some ragged ruminant's hide.

Despite occasional anger, she is the sway hip spine…
this town of dark eyes, sharp face & amiable understatement.

So I answer one day later
you can still go deep in familiar splendours
come back for air,
astonished & babbling.

Lake Pedder Lost[1]

1.
Over the browns &
ginger of that month.

Rain on the daygangs of
silver mist
loitered.
First light ink-brush fingers
combed the distance / soothe
the arch back of stone.

2.
They wait
for the word
in weatherblown, torn khaki plastic.

Torrents
in angry fusillade drop from the clouds against
the obdurate calm of the waters,
as like opposing elements
this downpour is no relation
to the lake's placidity
or the earthbound beard of ice that clings
brittle beneath overhangs.

Tears
& other human stuff
bounce off the pink sand.

---

1 This poem is set on the day damming of Lake Pedder began,
one of Australia's great environmental struggles & defeats.

3.

Some have dived to find the hidden shore,
pressed fingers on the beach.

& sunsets still bring rose to the water
as the lake lies buried beneath itself.   ⦿

Port Cities

The compradors in corridors
whisper like lions.
Capitalism's chicken or egg — what difference
everything is cooked.
Townfolk are owned by the sea,
land is just an addendum alongside death & children.
Bales house the mice of scholarship.
There were poems in the rafters
while down below trust slips by Customs regulations.

Water hands
& bags of rice — all
fears stink of fish.
The birds of message scour oily sand;
those true arts of acquisition & guano
cry out from sanctified towers.

Shophouses light joss,
smoke flees the market.
Down by the quay
beneath the calico of his visions
there's a flailing beggar on his throne of scraps.
Children run riot across 16 cultures
while all the wisdoms have left for a frayed inland seclusion.

Like the purple loosestrife & monkey flower
port cities are the waterborne seeds of nations,
needs & atrocity.
They bloom by rules that lords can't fathom.

In these brisk lives
borders are small things.

Surfside Ave

We sat around the kitchen table
a parliament of pleas.
Then a rat — huge —
almost the size of a possum
came through the louvred windows
& grazed the formica like an entitled guest.

Three damaged men lived there —
one abruptly jobless, another
Kawasaki-smashed on bitumen
the third so politely dropped
          from the One Great Love.

At the far end of the table
our cat watched us gravely
then nodded towards the visitor
who stood still as a commandment
over a loaf of bread.

This place — depending on the wind
you could hear the waves
or the roar of highway traffic.

A swamp out back
cackled in its busyness.
Some cloud pillowed in across
the slipped sky of a flawless but failing day.

Despite the upper body cast
Matt rolled a joint with a placid deftness.
I opted for cider as usual, bleeding condensation.
It has always gentled my head plus contains vitamin C.
Droplets caught the sunbeams & promised too much as

mosquitoes got dressed for work.
Our guardian spider primed her filaments
while neighbours argued at the dusk.

The cat yawned theatrically.
Each entity could see clearly
in opposite directions.
Something new, acoustic, seeped out from the speakers.
The paintings in the lounge were just sugar on the light.

There was no hope
so no worry.
That day refused to plan.
Perhaps immobility is grace.

Look Back in Languor

Summer never comes till January,
following the months of birth:
broken waters in a wet December,
the blood of xmas,
busy-ness of season. Then HERE.

Feet parade like dinosaurs on Bondi Beach wearing
gold from the granularity of sand
& lovers. We touch these grains as monks while
tour buses prowl the promenade a
revel in slow motion   (familiar in the dry notes,
                    dots amongst coils).

My thongs wander past
energetic panel vans,
& nearby, some anxious soul says
there is no fear   even as he looks.
He is an extra....
          (they also serve who only stand & stare).

She laughed *bang!* A woman, her fashion
falls as the promised leaves
falls like the surf,
like ink, like
something important.

Hormones above the droplets airborne, each day heat
hangs over everyone
like a loan.
The afternoon breeze arrives innocently.
Never, of course, to be trusted.

Children run across the placid surface of sunbaking adults,
someone thinks of dinner.
Hair teased up like parakeet, Matt, THE CORK,
does the heat...
all out there busy wet jets.

These clouds water-worn for us,
in a single bound, all different.

Small humours, pigment & the constant breaks.

Look back in languor,
        pure as idiocy
        happy as pharmacy

I ride the wave of your neck.
Ride this day.

The Ways of Waves

1. Stars

The beach hasn't slept.
He writes this
the wash against shore
like the spikes from the seaweed
latch & lose their grip
in the falling tide.

As cowled air, silver
& a grey feral coastline settles
in this layered murk
of a day before its birth

2. Toes

There is no part of our body more exposed as feet.

In one corner of the sky
                a leak of illumination.
Can feel his hair grow, the weight
of the bag & towel on his hands
like a fruiting tree.
Sees the ribbons of car light
ropes of surf.
He is alone to sort out tangles
but only touches the sand
a test for some fabric
rubbed between fingers   he lies down
to this chosen robe
& an approximate unity.

The sand is, after all,

just hanging around.

He reaches the water
& the grains bow away
as if help, servants
    leading the lost
to some great bed
    as unknowable as a pit.

Then at the bottom
listen to nullity, hands drift
in this new airless air
searching with a knife.

3. She Sleeps

By the sea there is a bed.
She turns & hair
& breast & arm
rise up on a disturbed moment
to smash back   spume
on the empty space
beside this lover.

4. The Knife

Was it always in his hand, wrapped in the towel
or marking some space
in that book he'd been reading?

When he opens his fingers he holds glories,
the weight of the world without effort.
So why this chrome splinter?

He kicks out deeper, till he & the surf fight.
Once past the breaks the steel is dropped &

a seed of murder is gone
from the air & from him.

New sunlight disinfects.

His lover waits in the safety
of duressed linen & the aureate morning.

5. Wholesome

She has feelings for this man.
He sits hunched over his breakfast
like haze around a peak hour.
Living with him
heat
to tender
to lost boy retreating.
The ammonia in argon nights
strung together/
pacing scratched floorboards, she

is uncertain in their small Bondi flat with
a TV, some clothes
tattered Indian mat.

Is herself both at & being a pit stop.
Her pal once said of a boyfriend
At least he doesn't hit.

So brushes her hair
without fear
as the waves below crash
then recede
&
so
on.

6. Nudge

Under late-morning sun
they add two more rectangles of colour to
that quilt of towels on the sand.
The temperature glides
a kite
through the whispers of peace.

They shed their asphalt-clothes, flap with
a lazy passion in the sea
then lie down in this Australian cathedral
to sip
nothing.

& as they drink
they lose
job interviews & murder & need.

Pretence is flotsam, awaits
the turn of the tide.
Their fingers mine the sand,
seeking only more.
Irregular beads of sweat are a second
liquid skin designed for formless futures.

Silence, not touching they meet somewhere
in that middle where we all seek
(but can't describe).

Somewhere at the fringes of our plans
when we gave up hope.
Somewhere in the pattern of touch & push.

That spot
where you change
& that day is there
& all around you
found.

My Bronte Beach

is the loudmouth in the waves singing *Summertime*.
It's actors, politicians,
pensioners & the kids — shockingly minus stuff.

This incursion of spring is the radius of white plovers,
glare swallowed by each wavelet
as a tourist biplane dissects the new cyan of midday.
In Sydney it gatecrashes (around now)
just for a moment
then winter never feels at home.
She will move out like some rattled tenant
on a short-term lease
in the rough part of an unruly town.
This beach — the dominance of birds
politely ignored by undercover dogs
pale skin
on raw sugar sand.

Someone known — just out of hospital —
totters back to the sea
a great aged turtle.
Cedars of Lebanese legs copse around BBQs.
A street-guy's washing dries on the memorial quartz as
buffed teenagers laugh like lawn sprinklers.

Community, the accretion of small tragedy
that attends every understood life. It's my wife,
on a seasoned wafer of towel, absorbed
by utter quiet. The sun disinfects.

Our unremarkable cottons are heavy by the shore
straight lines don't fit.
We don't own ourselves, but each one,
we all have separate Brontes.
The sand takes the shape of our need.

Tide

Kelp moves
in vast stretching strokes it's
colour dictated by competing
sun & shade hides
hives of life.

My silhouette too
is part of those
neutral but defining
spectral lines.

The immediate gut-peace on contact with the sea, still
my feet rest in steel, words connect
webless urban imagery...
round paintballs of purple coral, fingerlings
slice like machines across a Sanskrit of perturbed sand.
They are busy collecting
while a mighty blue groper moves
as part of some greater tide.

A round puckered scar on his side (a speargun's work?) matches
one on my shoulder caused
by sun & pierced ozone.
We exchange glances, but no understanding is possible.
Both wounded, we are genetic puzzles
pass on separate journeys
amid the tranquillity
& casualty
of a stolid ocean.

Our locomotion subsumed in a tumescent sea.

Milk Beach

Prayer is this discard basketball
washed up at the shoreline.

The poem is inside that ball,
air under pressure.

Tears require practice.

We are wrapped in poisonous bandages of summer.
As always
the cure is the punishment.
We build up   fall down
so can't be just flesh
though probably less
than the sum of our garbage.

All this beneath
a sniggering fig —
my list of miseries
is still just a sheet of paper
even my fingers keep saying
just like this.

No fish lose sleep over justice.
They are their own comfort, connection & cloister.
Beneath the call of muezzin ferries
each basketball is beached
in its very own moment.

Brighton-le-Sands

Bleach & blow-dry sand supports an argument
between three septuagenarian Macedonians.
I join in, the subjects are important —
politics & water temperature.
The sky refuses to take sides.

Sun wears skin
she's here for the medicinal salts. A magenta stingray
is finger-painting at the edge of this canvas sand,
it will take her some time.

That water is as clear
as paper waiting for the poem one never quite wrote.
Ignore the clouds out across the bay, the traffic —
it's just that cheap ambient mix that lulls all purpose to slumber.
This is my begging bowl,
the offerings of serenity while I am alive & pain is managed.
There is always risk in excessive marvel.
Like my *wealth & beauty* it's just a memory of names.
There are strategies
plus measured delusion does only a little harm.
Children collect driftwood
to assail so many magnitudes.
Dunes knell
at the altar of local government.

This frangible splendour has no contracts with time,
the air warms.
So near the airport,
all those furtive lives amongst the hooks
fish stare up at the planes:
they are the stars.
This bay goes all-ways

& I am stationary, fixed upon
the myths of departure & flight.
There's turnoffs just south a bit – *Canberra, Wollongong.*
As a ketch absconds towards the ocean
busses offer *Dolls Point* & *Sans Souci.*

My bicycle reluctantly took me north from Cronulla —
these things like dogs take on their owner's appearance —
loose screws & corrosion... a pitted grey writes notes at the sky.
My faith is a thorn, intent as gulls
I feed on other lives, wrapped just in a worn laugh.
This surfeit, the loss of shadow
& cantankerous memories crowd the bikelane.

Gods should stop their stubborn shine —
edges have sung at me for years, I've seen
colours you wouldn't believe,
my hurt filled the balloons of shame
to pass as an excuse.
This is now a diminutive world comprised of
cotton shorts & dabbed sunblock.
Perhaps if we all took it as sufficiency
there'd be the air to save.
To my left an A380 lifts from the tarmac
— miracles — you see what I mean.
I've got to stand for something
& this will do.

Shoal Bay

Bluebottles
the colourful disemployed are
washed up on the shore,
lethal & lazy beneath
waves that fall like a baby's pat.

I have a contract with the day & must walk.
The extinct volcano drools dolmens,
cares little for the struggles of flesh.

One day I passed a woman, said she was washing
but the bucket she carried was clouded
with curdled milk.
The magic wins in the pests' nests
& starling chicks have no manners.

Most tracks are the same but
leave one for a fortnight then there's
an overhead spray of arachnid-monstrosity black stars.
Freed from people, spiders spin a loose extravagance
over all open space.

By the creek
a sweep of mosquitoes — addiction (marriage
of syringe with vein) they're
flying forays through flailing hands
with a welcome humanity rarely receives elsewhere.
Come back come back.

One day walked by a child with a basket full of phlegm.
She stoops to harvest. We're all on different journeys.

The disemployed hang beach towels on verandas

their medieval banners, the business
& indolence of festival.

By night I am a stranger to myself
behind a tree,
splashed light by passing cars...
astonished *ahs* to each immoderate shadow.
I walk on a roof in dainty steps/
the ghost on a black'n'white TV/
branches fall during storms.

I've been making notes by the same headland.
A fire in a balloon, wearing
stone to instability.

Spy & spectacle are co-conspirators.
Time only exists through our eyes.

Off Highway

An outlandish splay of flowering clover like
a thick sundried sheet across
the Memorial Oval.

Dozen galahs &
three ducks are busy feeding, they
waddle like Bob Menzieses beneath
a clear impertinent sky-breathing air
that is true pure barring
the faintest whiff of petrol.

Down the street there is a clean row
of well-trained lawns only
"auction — Must Sell" falls apart
the grass well overreaches its pudding-cut obligations.

Okay, behind the occasional curtain
a syringe joins the dance.
Kids run away, down south to a Sydney
they see as an adult-type amusement park.

Recriminations accumulate like rusty junk in backyards.
They vote in a right-wing idiot.

It took Judith ten minutes to dismiss it as *suburban*.
Each street with its gutters going down to the bay —
orderly, lifeless rivulets.

Dependent on the wind, you
either heard the crash of waves
or the prop jobs from the local airstrip.

Judith said the place was *brain dead*

& I thought of her as I nod to each of the locals,
we shuffle past each other
like dinghies only pretending we weren't adrift.

Even the accents are different, they sound
just like us, out west
before the 'seventies
before I escaped to become
an *important person*
(a curse on those who still believe
in action as any
kind of answer).

Off the heads I snorkel.
The fish & I are
firmly placed
here.

There's a forgotten Australia by
the Lion's Club playground.
The community cottage
(*Wed. Gamblers Meeting, Thurs. Centrelink*)

No "time warp", no nostalgia
(they had jobs back then)
but I'll go a lap or two
in the council pool.

Not being
a cranky old fart
I balance armloads of past & future like that
harassed Parramatta bag boy I once was
crossing the main road to customers' cars,
dancing with steel.

Here I sit. Now.
Lost
but not uncomfortable.

Harbour Town

In this season I can only aspire to make trouble.
Wearing all my clearance clothes
I loiter at this bum-hole of winter
await any ending.
Constantly constant this
isn't peace or retreat, just *almost*.

Wind rifles up the coast
an indigenous flag falters
beside an invader's tomb of frigid marble.
The decommissioned sun joins the other homeless grifters.

Then September is ablaze.
Down on the docks trouble brews herbal tea.
The union refuses to concede
while I sail by in my excuse thimble
& count money.

This drags on as all things do
the season rots the fingers...
they'd held on through nasty months,
only now to compost alongside
eucalypt leaves & nest-fallen chicks.

City beaches abrade our pert decisions.
Drinking all the salt we craze about in lethargic elegance
until the drum solo when
DNA wakes the lovers up to tweak & rustle.
Silver eyes watch, reflect on water.

Belief Beach

Anchored in the treachery of sand
wearing waves
until the snip of a certain comber
shreds them landward.
They call this weed.

There are people here too
busy in their pleasure they stare further out
across the stolid hungers of tankers queued
to feed national necessity, rapacity.

Boardriders have learnt those arts of waiting.
One child, one gull, the pantomime of chase.

What comes next? No point to tint anxiety
on that small forest of eelgrass.
That's ours to bear, our curse.

A granite breakwater, that construct built on collapse
is the human pretence of permanence
a theology of safety...
that most friable of gods.

Below the surface
hardier energies persist.
Though lifeless, sand has its ructions.
Waves bustle in the frenzy above
they cannot be ignorant of the one before, the one after.

Deluded in the shifting breeze
(that is a life in itself)
one placid pensioner
will not go deeper than her knees.
She is content in the fake permanence beneath her feet
that is neither loyal nor solid
as it buries abandons undermines
all that is somehow held to be true.

Interpenetrating Gyres

When the captain gave up plunder
he began inscribing
a memoir of consequence
on the shell of a lime-green snail.

Carrying the burden
— those notes on the nature of treasure —
this marauding mollusc ate through
the passivity of upland forests.

Oaks, finding themselves denuded, withdrew their roots
& followed that hungry speck
back down to a river where a hymn of water-lilies
promised shelter in an end.

Staunch cattails applauded,
those trees with a century of project
discovered that all along they were lumber
hiding within their weak skin of life.

He had tried the pipe & cuddle
but our captain saw that truth bore a hardier carapace.
As logs bobbed up against his jetty
the crew returned, started building their next vessel

because this was the single path they recognised
even though it led only to atrocity.
There is epiphany here
but is it seaworthy?

Girilan

On Asian sand
this dozen bemused tourists surround a dead dragon.
Its last ferocity
is the stench that armours each ending.

Already delicate fins are trimmed to lace
by the scission of crabs.
Beneath a corona of flies
spirit is urged to shuck flesh.
Harp of teeth
reach out to voice.
A roadmap of spine leads towards the spume.
Hygienically cleansed
under flash–bulb asepticism
any shift in tide will send this
crashing to the tale.

There is history,

but it won't tell.

Puzzled

We are a difficult pestilence
cursed by intelligence
without silence.

The Beast Collective

Skitchem. The boy & the dog
have picked up this imperative, chewed it.
This command was built to be thrown,
has a bite deep in its vowels
& a snapped-off fang lodged in its k.

How did both come to know its meaning?
Like the word has some deeper source than mere
paper & repetition. Perhaps it is a fragment
from that original contract between us animals;

when a wolf came inside the cave
& our fire made instantaneous sense to it.

We will kill together. This bond will never end.

Immortal

1. Look

Arms control —
with those eyes hard as a wet winter beach —
you have no idea.

At 14, I worked in a store
where loitering pipe smoke prowled gun oil, licked

sharp edges of senescent inventory, frozen bait.
I was an ear in a male-only tooled-timber box of
casually rationed words.

Occasional weekends out on the property,
men with time,
their tinkering congregation of etched hands.
The smell of rolled cigarettes/
tree stumps blown away with a hand-made charge.
Posts planted, then wire braid —
cajoling the assumptions of sod.
Later, while pissing against the yard fence,
told the prudent rules of being grown up.
Breath crowded a bruised, shiver-night.

I remember the luger: a nazi, 50's movie grey…
snugly hosts an orderly queue of bullets
each immobile before its turn to replace the previous.
Malicious, fluid precision.

War surplus 303, a cannon on the shoulder.
Wilful as a workhorse, one had to be strong just to shoot the thing.
22s were the incessant kelpies;
followed you around, hauled everyone to a stop

at any rabbit, crow or fox.
Each weapon had a character,
its varnished name.

2. Feel (it)

The sweat-polished wood, eyes slip

on the judgment of schooled metal.
More sensual than love
with all **that** compromise & blunder.
Bullets & weapon sit ready, placid
even horny as fingers will brush
buttocks on statues,
cup a breast, the balls.
This is the best men can do
manufactured, calibrated,
sings under blunt fingers
then explodes
with a husked condensation of intent.

3. Taste

Sharpest in the memory,
a time beneath a hills-hoist north-coast sun
when Lenny & I were shooting air rifle slugs
just loose, up into the gums.
Until (colours implausible beyond the palette)
a thing of green & gold fell
clipping branches — rushed, heedless as though
this was the most important event in a life.

Then at our feet, a slapstick red
on its sunglass lime — heave of a tiny chest
slate eyelids locked.
That parrot demanded further butchery
to hide the crime & leave

a flat decency of death, the jury of worms.

Two small males learnt,
went down the hill in search of a spade
followed by creamcake hours
amongst the baked company of women.

We thought they knew everything
except our filth.

Carnal Knowledge

By 15 Giselle had run away from boarding school 6 times.
Woolloomooloo had the music *Summertime*
or so it promised. 1972, we bought the street
it wasn't cheap.
I let this old guy do me a few times, $50 a pop.
He always scrubbed his dick with Dettol afterwards
then showed me photos of his kids.

Love Hurts. No idea what I wanted,
she aimed to have sex with 200 people
before she was 18.
It seemed an impressive ambition.

The squat on Palmer St propped itself upright
waiting for inevitable motorways.
Matt & Dace were my best friends.
Knocked on their door, Giselle answered
naked & wasted. We hadn't fucked,
she said *It's Time* & wasn't political.

But I had gonorrhoea,
my bum black & blue from the shots.
She laughed, said "That's cool baby, I got crabs."
Was NOT going to happen.
We smoked some more
the music — a viscous organ
with emphysemic guitar —
something about *broken wings...*
so **there** we couldn't talk kinda
the normal state
Way down below the ocean.

Silent all those years
we met again last year at a launch.
She was an office manager
& grandmother, *Crimson & clover.*
Of course, we worried about our kids
in a tipsy, quietly confident way.
On the bus home two teenagers
Hakim & Adil (know them from the neighbourhood)
were defending the footballer accused of rape
"she's just doin' it for the money, dude"
then got onto the subject of consent.
Both weren't real sure
had a few ideas.
They'd been thinking about it lately.

The Table

Prudence is sedition.
The more you eat
the more you grow. Junk Economics.
Broadsheet liftout sections parade —
business, cars, travel...
a new career from slave yard
to auctioneer. People need their dreams
but why dress them
in trash armani?
Affluence. Cloud Nine — no humans, motorways
sleep in the park beneath
a teeming sky of continuous fireworks.
Spacious as friends,
our pinion of harvest...
the lazy or the ride.
Every man should have his lily
then set sail from the Cape of Storms.
I've aspired to
but did not try
nothing left.
Perilous absence makes the heart grow
puerile. Black simpletons,
the bereft adepts howl in their shelter
as we shake loose coins like wet dogs.

I know less each year
& cannot rise to judge.

™ Trade Marked

Bemilla wanted to be Barbie.
Surgeons removed each fold or blemish,
shoved in the curves.
Labiaplasty tidied up neat-nice
      electrolysis solved the hairy problems
         nipples were excised &
her feet were curled so she could never stand unshod.

This woman became what she loved
& aren't we all a little jealous?

But I wonder about thoughts that ran beneath the nylon coiffure.
Were there lurid pink pills
to tame all messy notions?
Was there anything *more* to be done?
How to stop,
an endemic predicament for everyone.

Tears have aquaplaned down her polished cheeks.
There is only a whiff of eternity —
this project denies time.
So will fail.
There are doubts, pastries & their consequence.
Those lips can be kissed too much
to a point where they crumple.

Perhaps she'll be remembered as a martyr,
we expect those at the edge to burn.
Whatever happened to is a verdict
but just as much an ambition few of us achieve.

One More Peace — 1991

Iraq. After this pocketful of time it's like the
memory of illness, reduced to anecdotes.

On television I remember the desert,
sliced neat as sandwiches by
paved arterial roads.
Above, the sky is clear
as the vision of the gods we confect.

The bad meat smell
that marks ex-humans. Those highways littered
like the playroom of some child antichrist.

Tell the story... "allied" planes
above their monuments of smoke...
some gasses reach through filters to
irritate the eyes of american heroes.

Why do I   despite the silence,
still fear this peace?

The World Is Sport

My primary school girlfriend
was the school's best cricketer.
I learnt my place
as she bowled me for a duck every lunchtime.

On the boy's high school's cross-country run
the indigenous kid Mick lurked in the gully,
beat us weaklings righteously
as we wheezed towards resolution across *his* land.

The school captain election was between the sports star,
the smartie & a pansexual anarchist matchbox-weed supplier (me).
It was no contest.

In Ulindu the President lands on the pitch by helicopter,
security fans out
& the national team stop training to accept honorifics.
Like, one is proud but scared shitless
better beat Ghana next week
or the promised new car could drive you to your death.
General Rala loves every minute,
these wars are cheap.

Flesh is a commodity.
Rich, indifferent men buy teams
& barrio boys all dream of exit...
the model wife, new teeth.
They bet their bones.

The arts enclave of every city has its physicalities —
feather-touch football, barefoot bowls where
teams are named after robust cabernets.

In Australian business, warming up to next big negotiation
in a sort of fiscal pre-match entertainment,
they discuss the latest team scores.
Men & women both, it's a glue to help agendas
appear to be indistinguishable.

There is an idea about
that we have grown too cerebral & lazy.
Worriers don't make warriors.
Always wearing their sunscreen
most modern Australian players
will never achieve a single good ferocity.

Paradice

Sunblock cream, tax evasion
Switzerland is so Australian

like Neil'n'Keith
an icy beer
bikini wax(ing lyrical)

An island   night doesn't fall,
it lowers
          like a bow
          like back problems like
it or leave it

as good as it's going to

as easy as it's ever

a little bit torn
& tethered.

Bright & Pure

Dressed in moths,
eternity.

Airy aviary
feed the pigeons
eat the pigeons. Peck at faith.
Trees came into the city, hungry.
Meat, cigarettes, toll-booths all concern
the roosting of energy.

Dappled, fickle days —
Katrina sings while drowning.
Humans are set here to injure & cure —
live with these split, spilt imperatives...
largely without question.
The man sat under those trees & planned his assault.

His cough comes bright as cherries,
feet crash in the clay,
shed cells to make
prayer mats. Each "deserves" so much
but not punishment.
He begs, then offends again.

Christmess

Work shall set you free
— concentration camp motto

1.
The sugar fed violence of this season, the
heat & company float.

John was smoking & drinking, thinking thirty
five was coming up fast & he was still inner
city flat $$$ per week & in the middle of
the year's 5th virus & 4th relationship.

His work was eating him. When it wasn't
they subtly questioned his sick days perhaps
counselling & his hair could/   decided
          whether to grey
          or go away.
He stopped the habits & thinned,
some days you'd swear he'd been skinned,
stripped down as he left his front door.

Last week he quit, a wine stain
          on the herringbone of life
     burnt out   no gold watch or those farewell
dinner speeches of another time
when people retired,

when suns had slowly cooled, not exploded.

2.
I started two months later at the same job, what
was exactly 3 years after Janet left me.
She eventually dropped normalities

for megabytes & coffee lounge deals, the Future,
where new cars appeared instead of children &
the million-dollar smile grew toned like gym.
Her crisp new husband & the
arrangements multiplied till her life was
64 alternate coloured squares
& Janet was tough ivory with just a
dash of liqueur.

3.

> *WE ARE THE GENERATION. Van Morrison*
> *will always be playing on our radio.*
> *In thirty years' time retirement homes*
> *will sprout jacuzzis*
> *& consultant naturopaths.*
> *I can already hear the cry*
> *TAX OUR CHILDREN*
> *know the reasoning will be impeccable.*

4.
Janet's talks about **doing music**, she's just been offered
the director's position, makes her horny & tonight
she'll ask someone to travel her *Country Roads*, invite someone
into her xmas stockings
        ]frankincense & mirth[hohoho riding
Santa's splay with bells while
she dreams about **doing music again**.

5.
This is a bleak xmas. Those with fuel
can keep it going 365 days a year. Please to god I want
to be a tree, not a rocket.

After I'm rich I'll do
two year's penance in a
Wilderness Society koala suit
                then escape to some farm near the beach

because I just buried a friend who
lacked the grace to die, she
got me that latest job where this tired
pretended indifference is clutched like bunny blanket.
My enemies madden —
a xmas wish answered
& last night I dreamt we all sat around a new born child.

To call us three wise anybodies, well,
you gotta laugh.

⬤

Mea Culpa

Today is full of no direction.
Rarely has been or perhaps
just impassable routes for me.
So stepped outside the honeycomb —
the air's so hard but
I hold on.
You can hug something long enough,
it becomes a simulacrum of loving & reprieve.

Pinned on the plateau of a nagging mortality
my breath is seized by hungry owls.
They dissect with a holy patience
until the bones of words clatter downtrack to
what used to be safety.

There was a book on bodies that I never read
(though am a co-author).
The fuss all dissipated
after lies were exposed.
I am richer now.

Local Hero

There've been too few *explanations*.
When I said there's no easy answer
& tried to apply it
only the trees agreed.
I was hung from one upside down
the mob thought belief would rush to my head.

But that head has long been overcrowded
so I was then forced to watch the news

> battles raged over parking fines
> our leaders did something criminal
> & the public just giggled at the scamps.

Oil bubbles up
though temporarily obscured by leaflets.
Demagogues roar as celebrities write prescriptions.
Waters rise, they taste of conclusion
& that would be the verdict we must wear.

But there's a joy in all this somewhere,
so many worlds
I think I lost one.
Layers can't be removed through self.
> Don't trust something you can't massage.
> Let love only leave you further lost.
> > Death is rumoured to be contagious,
> > tears are not a pollutant.
> > Plant. Question. Don't rush.
> Long walks by oneself —
> more than enough.

Off National Park Rd

Despite this morning's poorly named downpour
there is no falling at the waterfall
no pooling at this pool.

This day both placid &
adamant alongside unapologetic autumn — 25°.

I wish I could leave words to other people
me lacking both the succinctness of wandoos
& the promiscuity of the breeze.

A 10-year-old is shepherded past —
it's the worst walk I've ever had! But
I just wait for the zealous silence to return,
my reliable page.

The rust & glower of stonefell.
Undercolour staunch mantis green concedes to shabby linen.
Shade rations itself
& is infested with ants.
Does the shrike react when I say it is elegant?

There are shoots everywhere...
a cuneiform of life
beneath notice, against the odds.

I am thirst
& trespass.
One cannot rake the scrub into stanzas.
Could string together all the words I have
& the magpies would still think themselves uncaged
or at least have no notion of boundary.

Envelopes won't seal the wounds,
feet haven't got the rhythm
& my sweat is tasteless.

Wind Instruments

*I honestly believed that the world was about to come to a crossroads, where
money, war & society were all about to be forever altered. In the face of that
absolute inevitability, the most logical thing seemed to sing. After all that time
I've yet to come up with a better idea.* Robin Williamson

We still look for Licorice McKechnie.

After the band broke up
of course she went to america.
Could be dead but almost certainly
somewhere west, the tumbleweeds
of faith curl the sands —

but Leena & I were there, she didn't show.
We called across arroyos
wrote in highway dust.
There was only a little cash.
Summer shrieked its blues, haboobs
had been practicing... the slide —
that puke & grit assail the dunes like murder.

Our hungry cars chewed on beetles,
hopes went to shade & assumed a passive menace.
We couldn't approach her most likely hangout,
the laneway was too damaged.
Perhaps Licorice had the love's dementia,
Arizona does that
to any mild holiness.

So much smoke for just a few coughs of poetry.
Our irrelevance is durable,
effortless to maintain.
Freedom actually is free, but hazardous.
An email came in from Joshua Tree, California.

Backroads were renamed after decades
or abandoned, overgrown.
Joan is still busy. Jansch has gone. & Martyn.
Sting has a vineyard in Tuscany.
Arlo votes Republican.

For myself, I try
to put out a *collector's item* every three years —
more feathers come in than royalties.
I have no complaints
while I search for Licorice McKechnie.

The Love-It-Till-You-Don't Club, Cutcliffe

Terry. Vietnam.
That word is all that is necessary, they
cured the cancer. *Big deal.*
With his Seniors Card rode the bus to pick up Nembutal.
For years he felt there was magic yet in his world, plus
he lived near the beach.

Friends will be there
but by obligation "not there" -
this loving called death must legally be done in solitude.
Booked into the Sunshine Motel.

He belongs to a group that helps their members live & die.
Never too much pain, nor much joy
he remembers the boy he was
& apologises at the air.

Medicine can be tougher than the patient.
Lost his way at Falldown Bay.
Never *too much* pain.
Those who cared flapped about him pesky precious,
orbited his damage for years.

There were pinnacles in his life.
Marlene & her hippie dresses,
she could tea away apocalypse.
Cowboyhat Hannah just got to scootin'
as Daisy went & flowered straight out of the garden.
It's not that it matters, small tears
in a tattered t-shirt. They were all so piss-weak
& twice as strong as him.

Not a dole bludger,
that pride above disability.
Mate/employer Davo says
he can't cope without him
(should never have been a builder anyway).
Davo whinges a lot, reckons he's just a man
fighting depression, custody, bankruptcy but
he never *served*.
Terry *served*, knew a few miracles.
Still shrugs, thinks *big deal*.

Slip away, this day.
People will drop by around 7pm, check there's no pulse.
The road to well is sometimes a dead end.
Call box notification to police, because those
hard-pressed cleaning staff aren't paid enough for bodies.
Terry will be honoured, a forward scout again, trailblazer
in the territories beyond hurt.

The Euthanasia Workshop

Mark & I have both seen ghosts.
For two agnostics a surprisingly comfortable realisation.
But no ghosts today,
I sit with dozens of 60 70 80 somethings
all eager for gossip from the express bus to dust.

There are hugs from friends, how come
so many repeat attendees?
Are they checking on who're still around
their pre-purchased poison wrapped in foil
on the fridge door shelf beside the mustard?

While Esther thinks her heart pills will do the job
Barry's bought the nitrogen kit online with
(of course) a *recyclable* plastic bag.
Mexico has Day of the Dead veterinary bus tours
while a civil Chinese online supplier
called Smith is *100% genuine.*

When I run across a colleague at the tea-table
we both bluster *Knowledge is power* yeah right.
Seems like demise is the last challenge...
one has climbed mountains
& surfed that stupid-huge wave off Oahu.
We frocked & balding adventurers
won't be pushed, we'll jump.

Even modern death has such a hurry
no time for cupcakes & pretty monologues.
There's much laughter —
especially when we hear Grace's rehearsed last speech
was short-circuited by the fast reaction.
Her last words for posterity —

this tastes like shit.
No way Nembutal can pass as a cocktail...
our final sip has disgust built in but
right to the end life costs,
there's always an aftertaste.

Peace

Pipped at the epiphany.

The Compassion, Rut & Self Proposition

There's news just in from neuroscience
& it's not pretty.
By some scholarly criteria we don't exist.

Music is a tingle in the nucleus accumbens
right between the eyes
but no one can truly hear or see.

Circumstance, experience is data. The soul
is a sweeper for the mind which
fools itself or with itself the difference:
breadth of a blade.

Thalamo-cortical system collects the toll thinks itself
motorway though it's just a lane that feeds elision.
Our complicated machine, the cheating circuitry
so busy but creates only those baubles
& babbles we call insight.

Violence at a distance satisfies completely.
After everybody worked hard to make them,
those sweating divinities in their beach cottages
have no option as they spray supplicants
with their briny amnesties.

There's deceit in each choice, psychiatric hygiene.
Forget your education.
Crippled primates on a new tangent
have fallen from the trees into office cubicles.
Ali al-Sistani says Quran okays
masturbating in front of one's wife
so long as she helps.
Torah lets you eat locusts, but not oysters.

Look at those switches —
the processing of speech, facial recognition,
social emotions like shame, disgust — click click.

The occipital lobe censors out
rubbish streaming in through eyes
that wear their black spots like a promise.
Consciousness — that narrow light,
flange of brain — a frilly dress for agony, desire.
Therese swears pertly, symmetrical bones —
just looking at her lights up reward centres.
She's thinking about work the next day
as Allen's conditioned rape response kicks in.

Amygdala screams as easily… all connected —
polysemy pile-up towards the narrowest of consensus.
We're perhaps cabling & fluids
senselessly cooking in the brainpan, bubble'n'squeak.

Accelerant intellects across the globe ignite tiny suns
yet still are astounded by xmas lights…
toddlers & meddlers all of us. The defence presented…
what else would one expect
with those lopsided cranial hemispheres.
We're mostly lethal to ourselves,
our old & damaged, new & selected.

Friends reinforce the collage of fiction that we are.
Addicted to praise, we grasp for one sure thing.
Like vigilantes we preserve
these flintier figments… burn through cities
to keep us reliable, right.

Certainty is a variety of lunacy.
A peer buys the drink

then you are reassured
effervescence in the beer, you are so *here*.
Boss gives you honey,
you drown in it.
No sin, only synapse.
To eliminate surprise
psychologists promise deep but they are
orchids high in rainforest boughs,
way above relevancy.

Identity scaffolds are up
but nothing gets built it's
about the scaffolds. The dorsolateral prefrontal
takes you for a night out
under the town.
Eccles' World 3 stops talking to World 2.

We're all on the blood bus
& you can't trust this
incident we call being. Bundle Theory, each one of us is a crowd.

Create a bright side.
Let all the philosopher/neurologist nit-pickers
lurch about this implacable complexity.
A new connection, a lubricant,
allows the wounded to wobble
towards the end of life with
fantasy padded around their every tumble.
Humans, whining death-sacks all,
shuffle through their moves.

But but but
optimists putter like two-stroke engines
towards the affirmations outside this argument —
those anagogic mountaineers.

The Empathy Trick has tiny audiences in tears.
You say *what about our kids!* I go all
softy gooey nest-mess so
pre-programmed & evolutionary.
We defecate predictability.

Doctors snip & a handful are silenced.
But shucking their unisex scold's bridle
others ride beyond conviction
to a knowledge deep in meat.
Parmenides' juggles-full of zeros,
Anselm's absolute good & perfection in a notion.
The flotilla of words show a certain flexion,
we are clever within our cage.
Free will, though never free,
can free. The next step
could be a revelation.

Small charges ignite a numinous spurt.
This can become a fountain, look!
The day after deluge
we abandon our homes for sandscapes,
white corellas croak like consumptives
a frantic pair of currawongs feed their craze of family.
This is no black/white binary no leaf/sky absolute.
Neighbours stand in gawk beneath simpleton sunshine
as it burns this small globe pure.
That awe, if swindle, is worth any *cost*.
Which is also imaginary anyway so why worry?

Then there is the brainchain.
Maria's thoughts beam out,
she touches strangers. This neural brushfire is perpetual
& a world-changer. If each self is a cascade,
an almost random deluge,

what is our community of selves?
There is an inundation of hatching outcomes —
all potentials, all hope.
Despite rats in the eyes,
Dan's patience has cured Stephen's hurt
& thereby cured himself.
A sacrament sits within simply listening.
That succession of aware entities that we are/will be
is a gift, a harvest.

Neurotheology — god is in giggles.
It is the hymn within our Personal Delusional System.
Neuroplasticity — we can sculpt a future with
our laughter, invent tranquillity
or dance with fairies. Irrepressible glory —
I will lay down my life to pretend it matters.

If it's all just blips
then that makes our sorcery a perpetual surprise.
There is yet more
sounds like a prayer,
I built my churches about this murmur
(though the conniving cortex *would* say that).

Ascent

It's a click in the head
shunt in the marshalling yard as carriages come apart
small ruptures
in the weeds of ganglion.
Then I fly.

Like a surfboard
but less devious turbulence
no chafe
or clutter of the mob.
The air supports
& insinuates.

No flap of imagined wings
or contraptions that ordered minds can fabricate.
This is me
without the gravity,
habits of the feet.

A mind let loose —
one part reads atmosphere maps
thermal tracks
gossip of jetstream.
The rest gasps with unlatched eyes
at human life made tiny —
a mosaic of congregation.

There is no distance, though touch becomes
a convention dropped along the way.

This is the time most alive
though I suspect I am asleep.
That stuff of bodies & the real
is a debate left adrift.

I wait
(some steps closer to empty space)
for solar flares, epiphany/
a collaboration of cockatoos.

Or the southerly change to send me
crashing back to flesh.

Adjustments

The People dreamt those mountains
that cowl their morning wakening.

Square off the horizon
a lake with its predation & placidity —
all the work that People must do.

I saw a jaguar amidst the trees...
pine, cedars all to be manufactured
to house & heat the civilisations.
That cat plucked orchids,
threatened all because
what worth is a plan once blotted
with wildness or beauty?

Martyr

It was the succession of concession
& the absence of quiet.
Blame the honest rage of pedestrians
as swallows fly past.

Each is born to wait
but only so long, have
X hundred hours, then jettison —
a surge of illumination or despair.
Some recharge afterwards
but the battery
is worn.

We are not tame budgies
serene in our memories of play & buffet —
more like wily ravens
picking at every lock.

The widow wired herself up
for her father's futile war...
yes, for paradise
for the son to university over in Tehran
for money
& the immoveable understanding
that this was her last queue.

This woman is no hero, dupe or monstrosity.
Each of her victims are a separate,
difficult puzzle. But we've all been somewhere nearby.
Let it go.

A small, fast bird
in her own conflagration.
She was wind across the sea,
discarded gristle

& if not hope, an end to hopelessness.

What's Saved

Fruit bats fall dead from the trees
        magpies hurl their barren nests
Then cinders become our new black.
Carbonised leaves are the last filigree.

Cities burn.
The air is overcoat grey,
sometimes when bushfires are nearer,
              shit-smeared apricot.
These are the last colours left.

A spitting rain hits soil, there's no permeation...
runoff scribbles obituary all down towards the town drains.
Even fire lost interest as it rooted about
the debris that thinks itself *forest floor*.
Feathers hide in soot. Fur sits in dismal clumps
& this is no seasonal moult.

Saw Steve last week
        to know titans tire.
He's been most of season out of town at fire fronts
to a point where the land wears his sweat
& he carries the smoke home to his partner.
Peter says he loves the solitude
but misses his man's hands
when he's absent or just back, exhausted.

Woodchips are fashionable this year,
concrete paths don't burn
but occasionally I find something...

Beside the Road to War

Like a currawong's wing
combing tangles of air
or the pulse of waterskin on this sated lake
        let me be lazy.

Beside the bat-squeal shift, pitch fruits of a roosting tree
twigs accrete by the hand's-span brook...
a minute dam of tadpole consequence.
White cockatoos weed, grumble —
we cannot ask for still
        so let me be lazy.

Stock markets crumple then soar,
money gibbers around the globe.
Roads stretch to fit our waistlines
as soldiers camp on contended land.
The Cyrillic of white
on the black swan's wing
is no battle plan for any general.
        But my eyes are indolent,
        those paths won't crack the world.

A cranky call from the water hen to planes overhead
then I am back amongst gesticulated argument
still based in the caves —
"we need more", "they want ours". Greed & Fear again.

Willows trawl the lake,
eels archive the histories of mud.
Time to replace the tribal gods —
they've started & won every war.
The Peoples of the Book[1]

---

1 Islamic phrase for followers of the three Abrahamic faiths.

should throw those books away.
There comes a time when blood
outweighs the ink.

I have painted all the pretty specks
done the overstand, then
the understand... without illuminates or audience.
My father is dead,
let the wet-coal tortoises mind the plinth;
we'll sing our hymns to fish.

A seagull whisks a cloud in the shallows —
your sleep is disturbed! You're lunch!
What surrounds us is not serene.
Crows are singing *Little Lamb*, each
weed is a contest.
But it's the violence of the blinking eye, hum of the skin.

Chain each man of power to weathered wooden benches
until the infusion of birdcall subdues their hands.
Immobilised eyelids will surrender
to a day of casual forage.

It's simplistic to say
simplistic to deny
we need peacekeepers
to patrol our heads. With *lazy* as our prayer,
train ourselves to say *enough*. Intelligence will listen
as each day becomes
its own statement of intent.

Ideas

A colour box had broken open
while furniture awaited delivery.

What is a husband?
When dies the weather?

They worked at personal growth,
the neighbours only saw mindless rutting.

Babies appeared from everywhere,
that need was a cacophony.

If all the missiles have use-by-dates
why don't they get used?

It was, after all, chemicals. Nothing matters,
so in pieces both our protagonists still exhibit their wreckage.

Critics were impressed
but no one bought the leavings.

Don't look. Please.

Struck

After we candles met it was decided to ditch
any tricks of the light.
Same table, each month
with our wax spread & conjoined to form
a museum of our previous couplings.

Thought we were romantic, subtle even.
Already paid.
No matches needed, we'd
self-ignite as waiters flapped unheeded
past our buffet of shadows.

The League of Legendary Women

Don't think their shields are mirrors.

I adore their fierce white teeth,
my women roar.
Face paint shatters on a belly laugh,
they plot with a potted glare
then march on down the stair without
wobble, wander or weave.

Cloaked in the convoluted cloth of fire & desks;
won pride. Strange, strange partners
they adopt their wounds.

No wife, maid, no nun or mum is tamed;
their neck sometimes submits
while brain punches back.
We strutting sons stomp blithely on perilous parquet.

There's more you say,
you'd be right. Hold them to your ear
then hear the gibber of the waves. Crazy as men,
contentment is suborned intent. They are everywhere,
like headlights randomly illuminate as they move
& sometimes choose to shine on you.

Three Rail Workers

In the signal box, elevated
beyond tracks, freight or people
Jack was smoking
& espousing
like a great steam engine while
Neal just sat quiet, his
body so at ease it was as if
the different parts chattered to each other,
shooting the shit.

I was younger, more stories
than scars.

& Jack pulled up a bottle from
that busted brown leather bag he took everywhere.
A few loose sheets of paper
were caught up in his hand along
with the bottle &
it seemed they hung onto that bourbon
like a bunch of desperate men.

But one by one
each page
dropped back
into Jack's sack.

There was a quiet to the place, each
bell or mechanical chnk discrete & isolated
so that by themselves the noises barely registered.
Up the tracks

an express freight stood at the 2nd Home with
the patience of some sedated circus elephant.

Neal wrote a haiku with his huge (caress) right hand.
Took Jack's reduced bottle
to his kissable lips.

Nervous amongst elders
my jokes aim for original
but often just "off".

I was the first one to break, that
train's power held back by only
the insubstantial
fakery of rules, coloured lights.
Pulled the lever & that locomotive began its
tectonic shift towards momentum as
the bottle sunk to the desk.

Jack scrawled the time in the signal box log.
He was always the recorder.

Boy lacks staying power Neal mutters.
I take up a tin of oil & a scraper —
leave to clean the points.

Jack smiles,
his pages writhe in the murk.

Emily Takes Off

The surgeons wanted to cut them out
but the girl had other ideas, albeit
half-formed like those lumps on her shoulder blades.
Scans were inconclusive
but the medical profession poked-prodded to a point where
bruises blossomed across her back.
There were suggestions surgery
could leave a tattoo of suffering
across her adult life...
all within acceptable boundaries
drawn by those without affliction.

As the skin began to split around
the urgencies on her scapulae
doctors sought orders from the court.
Her parents took the family on an extended holiday.
Process servers fretted about the vacated home but
all the neighbours refused to answer questions —
common good, common purpose.

Emily's wings required adaptation
but she thrived above the clods of debate, that
aggregate of rules, those
endless line markers at their bitumen.

Her party-dress of clouds now skims the globe.

Mooray

You wipe & wander
through a maze of trails stretched with webs as
though you were cutting a ribbon,
some official opening every few metres.

You stomp & wobble
through loud silence,
the cicada & whip of corella light/
sky cut spear of the Gymea Lily, speckled
craze of Christmas Bush in bloom.

You amble & stumble
till you reach a camp site, the
haphazard fireplace ringed with cans & stubbies,
some miniature Stonehenge.

Worn dirt, exorcised ash.
Tribal paint suggesting
Doug loves Linda
yet this scene
throbs with a history
of subtlety & excess.

I'll let any stranger
in on our people's tiny secret.

Between Big
Pineapples, Prawns & Rams we really
come to worship at the smaller,
hidden edge
where the weft of eucalypt scours the air,
its leaves stain ponds
to a sleepy tea that lulls us —

knowingly or not —

all to peace.

Tilt

At the edge of that cliff
every cliff
there's a wrinkle in the heart.
Feet argued amongst themselves.

To drop like a seed into unknowable...
but then I turn back
towards the approved certainties of my cabin.

How far can you go
into over beneath
the granite precipice of tomorrow?

No doubt in the end —
so much to do, to forgive, to touch.

Each cliff I pass thus far
they ask.   An answer —
I have enough.

The Avalanche

Daily he added stone to his garden.
As winter spread its infection the walks were shorter
his bones fought nerves up towards the peaks
that he would never reach again.

His daughter came by
worried at this new obsession.
Was it the mind
that truly wandered?

He worked beneath the shelter of his plan as
pitiless months held back the spring.
There was the chock & rattle of the yard,
scree of a life.

Not one casual choice.
What is living if not *method*?
One day it might be a polished pebble,
the next a splinter from the bones of Green Hill.

After a while, less talking to be done.
Why explain any obsession
amongst a species so cluttered with them?
In his trees, the birds repeated themselves.

His corpse was found smiling amongst flowers
that had defied the flinty impossibilities of his yard.
A last season had erupted as breath fled.
They now knew each memory had mortared his cairn.

Put Simply

Got up from my meditations,
had half a hash cookie
& an *Old Lions* gin swindle.

Played some music
then watched *Natural Born Killers*
from end to beginning.

It was so cold inside
the possum shared a laksa with me
then loaned me his coat.

The Earth has fallen.
I should have stayed quiet...
admissions like these only hasten decomposition.

Enough

There is no mail today
no prizes or bills. Let's be easy.
A kookaburra sheds down
like coins on a crowd of one.

It is raining somewhere else
& time won't finish yet.
Over breakfast
a light northerly wind grooms
crimson rosellas. Joy is deceptively busy.

For every pain there is a tablet.
Fish are reported back
in a once-polluted river. They pulped up trees
to bring me the news
but we hope small crimes are forgiven.
Wrioting opens the pores. This is not the end.

The back-bone's connected to the
sky-bone. The wish-bone's connected
to the home-loan.
Drinking greywater my
frangipani struts with flower.
Cloud's gone a bit toey but
yesterday a humpback whale came close to the shore
phones clicked agog &
all be well.

Personal Best

After watching hilarious videos of kooky animals
in the bosom of my Facebook buddies
there's that ardent ad about late-life flab,
car alarm going off down the street
& thoughts posted about "Peak of Life".

A journalist threw the notion on young Dan
who starred in a local-content soap
until he was scripted to marry & die
in a motorcycle accident season finale.
He was plucked from celebrity
like a stray grey hair. His future —
an apprentice plumber (no small outcome).

As a teenager,
to avoid being beaten up as the school brainiac
I deliberately fudged my answers at the final exam.
Miscalculated, relegated the next year to the B class.
The principal told my parents I had sadly peaked early
but would find something to do in my adult life, *something*.

The crooked bones of a dancer I knew
beat her down to the wretched humility of a saint.
Now with great paucities
she gives so much — her help, her desiccation.

Christine has burnt through university,
won all the prizes.
Ron has money plus a social conscience
which sits pristinely unused in his drawer,
he's *ready*.
Having lived a few more years I know
whatever they do each
comes to their own disaster naked under floodlights.

Then later as survivors
we wheel our wounds towards friends' backyards,
or down to the river swimming hole... float
deliriously empty as aquatic predation churns on
beneath our laughter & belief.
Perhaps I *peaked* when I bought my 5th suit?
Those salesmen of zeniths had promised more.

I don't think much about summits, I see a range.
Ghastly, glorious mountaintops & plummets array
both before & forward.
We should all be mountaineers,
plant the flags, our lists of awe...

> See a toddler babble with insight.
> To have watched someone die.
> Have your defeats (nearly) as welcome as the wins.
> Accept mercy.
> Deny mercy & be okay with that.
> Know your comfort zone is a prison cell,
> > step outside it
> > > then go back in.
> Know love & muck it up. Forgive yourself,
> > be forgiven.
> Blow on love, how those flames come back.
> Give up on the hard work —
> > certainly most hatreds.
> Live to a time when people regard
> > your hang-ups as eccentricities.
> To have the dignity
> > to dismiss one's indignities.
> Know hope as the only engine,
> > run it mercilessly.

For me, the climb tomorrow.

Left to Our Own Devices

All this is true
to or by me
perhaps that friend.
In bits & pieces
masked to prevent damage
sometimes complicit, always watching
       solace   apology.

Once more I close the door, nestle
in a shady wound.
Here in Surf City life is hard
but we're in it for the ride, there's
a hungry little boy
with a runny nose
in the gateaux.

Lazy? Those stars barely fall.
The universe doesn't spin, it rolls over.
Not much to lose
our world can hardly end
with this line still unwritte

Acknowledgements

This project had its beginnings during the
Established Writer's Residency at the
KSP Writers Centre, Perth, 2019. The author is most grateful.
https://www.kspwriterscentre.com/

Versions of poems in this book have been published/broadcast from 2019 in *14 Festival Mundial de Poesia de Venezuela* (VE), *Antipodes* (US), *Ashbery Project* (US), *Australian Poetry Journal, Backstory, Between These Shores* (UK), *Blue Nib, Cao Tang* (CN), *Canberra Times, Chair Poetry Series* (IN), *China Business Daily* (CN), *Communion, Covidioms* (IE), *Eureka St, Feministanbul* (TR), *Festival International de Poesia de Medellin* (CO), *Fifth International Festival of Poetry & Liquor* (CN), *Four W, Human Rights Arts Festival* (US), *GeneSiir Festival* (TR), *Gold Dust* (UK), *I Can't Breathe* (KE), *In Your Hands, Kerala Literature Festival* (IN), *La Voce dei Poeti* (IT), *Live Encounters* (ID), *Messages from the Embers, Musings During a Time of Pandemic* (KE), *Otoliths, Pinecone BigO, Poetry in Multicultural Oceania (NZ), Poetry in sDreaming* (IT), *Poetry for the Planet Anthology, Politics and Prose in D.C.* (US), *Post Colonial Text* (FR), *Presence: Live Poets' Thirty Years at Don Bank, Remixt* (US), *Rochford St Review, Singing in the Dark* (IN), *Stand* (UK), *Stylus, Survision* (EI), *Text, Tinfish* (US), *Unexpected Visitor, Unfurl, Verge, Verity La Embody, Vessels of Love, VTV* (VE) *& War & Peace.* Work in this collection was nominated for the *Best of the Web* 2019.

My thanks to them all.

I send my smile & undying gratitude to some individuals who have been daft enough to get involved in publishing my earlier books: (A-Z) Linda Adair, Phillip Hammial, Richard Hillman, Christopher Kelen, SK Kelen, Chris Mansell, David Musgrave, Ron Pretty, Mark Roberts & Yury Zavadsky

IM Bill Farrow, Rae Desmond Jones, Avril Judd,
Mark S Leabeater, Bill O'Brien, Jutta Sieverding,
Billy Marshall Stoneking & Lesley Walter

www.ingramcontent.com/pod-product-compliance
Lightning Source LLC
Chambersburg PA
CBHW030920090426
42737CB00007B/264